Godmother

Godmother

An Unexpected Journey,
Perfect Timing,
and Small Miracles

Odile Atthalin

SHE WRITES PRESS

Published 2017
Printed in the United States of America
Print ISBN: 978-1-63152-172-0
E-ISBN: 978-1-63152-173-7
Library of Congress Control Number: 2016963734

For information, address:
She Writes Press
1563 Solano Ave #546
Berkeley, CA 94707

She Writes Press is a division of SparkPoint Studio, LLC.

Names and identifying characteristics have been changed to
protect the privacy of certain individuals.

"On ne voit bien qu'avec le Coeur."
—Antoine de Saint-Exupéry,
Le Petit Prince

To my Beloved Spiritual Guide,
and Constant Companion.

And for Gabriel, my Godson.

Contents

Chapter 1

My Noel Story, Winter 1943

"Love is in the one who loves, not in the one who is loved." —Plato

It was the year 1943. The Nazi army had occupied Paris and half of France for two years. We had moved to Normandy. Before the war we lived a very comfortable life in Paris, where I was born. Before the war and after the war, that's how we kept track of time. After the war, we would return to our Paris home.

We had to leave Paris. My mother hated the German occupation, seeing German soldiers everywhere grabbing the best of everything. Everyone lived in constant humiliation, fear, and outrage, and my mother could not tolerate it any longer. And it was hard to raise four kids, ages seven, five, four, and two, on very meager food tickets, unless you bought food on the black market, which my mother, although she could have afforded it, would never do.

Why Normandy? My father's parents, wealthy upper-class Parisians and landowners, had a family country home, called "Le Château" by the locals, in a remote part of lower Normandy, about sixty miles inland from the coast.

The estate comprised acres of forests and rich grazing land, including three farms and their farmers raising herds of cows, where we would get our milk, eggs, butter, cream, cheese, and even meat at the annual killing of the pig. Plus there were big vegetable gardens and apple, pear, and plum orchards. We used to spend one summer month there every year. My mother had become familiar with the farmers and their families. In 1941, the family mansion having been confiscated by the Germans, the farmers helped her find a small house for rent on the outskirts of a nearby village called Les Aspres. We moved in, my mother, the four kids, and our nanny, while my father kept his job in Paris.

In Normandy, a whole new life started for me. By then I was seven years old, the eldest, a strong, capable little girl, serious and a good learner, thoughtful and quiet.

In Paris I had gone to a big private Catholic school, where I wore a uniform, went to chapel every day, and after school walked, holding Nanny's hand, straight back to our home apartment.

My life in Paris was structured and supervised, while here in Normandy I had lots of freedom. I went to the small village school by myself, walking over a mile of dirt road through woods and meadows, rain or shine. I skipped down the hill, then across the creek in the middle of the village, walked up the hill on the other side, and arrived at school warm and exhilarated. We had only one mistress for twenty kids, all in the same room. I could memorize anything, poems, songs, history, math. Our mistress loved me and I loved school. I discovered how much I liked doing things on my own.

"*Tu es devenue indépendante,*" my mother said and seemed pleased. The move had been a boon for me.

As for my mother, she was pregnant again, her fifth pregnancy, although she was only twenty-nine years old.

She kept talking about it. I had become her confidante. In Paris my mother had her fashionable social life and had no need for me. She had no time and no interest for her children. The nanny did all the caring. Here in Les Aspres my mother was alone. In the village everybody knew her and she knew everybody, but she had no friends. She was from Paris, and most of them had never been to Paris.

She talked about the baby she was carrying all the time. She wanted a boy. She did not want another girl.

"The first girl was OK, one daughter is good, *ma petite Odile*," she told me, "but three more girls," she sighed heavily.

"I want a son," she repeated over and over again, "*un garçon . . . un fils . . . je veux un fils.*"

She was cranky, often upset, yelling at my sisters and also at our nanny, and even at our cook.

"He is getting heavy," she said, holding her belly. "He is kicking, he is going to be a strong boy. One more month," she added. She always said "he" when she talked about the baby. Soon he would be born here in the house; the village midwife would come and assist her. She prepared the crib. She showed me all the baby clothes she had saved from the previous baby, my third sister, who was only two years old.

It was late October, getting cold and damp. When I walked back from school, it was almost dark, and I always came in through the kitchen door. Before I could step in, our cook shouted, "*Enlève tes galoches.*" (Take off your boots.) Then she gave me hot milk with chicory. I sat at the kitchen table. The kitchen was the warmest room in the house, except for the nursery room where my sisters stayed with our nanny. My mother came to the kitchen, sat with me, and started talking about the baby:

"*Tu vas avoir un petit frère*," she told me. (You are going to have a baby brother.)

And the cook repeated, "*Oui, ta maman, elle va avoir un petit garçon et toi t'auras un petit frère.*" (Your mom is going to have a little boy, and you will have a baby brother.)

Soon it was November, time to set up the crèche. Every year my mother would build, on a table, a small mountain with pieces of cardboard, and add a few rocks and twigs from the garden. Inside the mountain, she made a little cave, and inside the cave, she placed the small statues, the same every year, *les santons*, as we called them. There was Mary, Joseph, a donkey, an ox, a few shepherds, and a few sheep. Between Mary and Joseph, there was a small manger; it was empty. The *santons* were all staring at the empty manger. They were waiting for the baby to arrive, just like us. We were all waiting for the baby to arrive.

Every night, before going to bed, we gathered around the crèche, staring at the empty manger, just like the staring *santons*, and we sang:

Venez Divin Messie,
Sauvez nos jours infortunés
Venez Source de vie
Venez, venez, venez.

(Come divine Messiah,
Save our unfortunate days
Come source of life
Come, come, come.)

I already knew this song. Every year in December we sang the same song at my Catholic school in Paris and every night at home, so I could sing all the verses by heart. My sisters just sang the refrain.

When they had gone to bed with our nanny, I asked my mother, "What does it mean, '*Divin Messie*'?"

"It means someone very special," my mother told me. "Mary is pregnant, she is going to give birth to Jesus, he is special, he has a mission. When he grows up he will bring peace and happiness to everybody."

"Just like you, you are just like Mary," I replied. "You are waiting for your baby, just like Mary."

She laughed, rearranging the *santons* in the crèche, and replied: "Yes, I am waiting for my first son, like Mary, and he is going to be very special too."

"He will be special because he will be a boy," I added to show her that I knew only a boy would be special, "and that will make you really happy."

Every night when we sang "*Venez, Divin Messie, venez, venez, venez,*" I thought, *my mother will have a boy, like Mary, and that will make her happy.* I really, really, really wanted her to be happy. So I closed my eyes and I sang with all my heart. I imagined her baby was the *Divin Messie* who would make us all happy and bring peace to our family and to the village people, and to the people in Paris, and we would finally be happy. My mother said I had a nice voice.

One afternoon in late November when I got home from school and opened the kitchen door, instead of "Take off your boots," our cook screamed at me, "It's a boy!"

"What boy?" I asked, shocked by her voice.

"Your mom, she had a baby boy! Go and see him!"

"Where?" I asked, still confused.

"In her bedroom, she is in her bedroom. Go and see her."

I was so stunned I just stood there, so she grabbed my hand and took me upstairs to my mother's room. My mother seemed asleep but when she saw me, she sat up, and leaning toward the crib, she said, "It's a boy! Look, look at him. There he is, a baby boy, a perfect little boy, can you see him?" as she pulled the sheet down.

All I could see was my mother. She was so excited, and she was laughing and giggling like my girlfriends. I had never seen her like that before. My mother had become happy.

My father managed to come from Paris for a few days to see his new son, quite a job as trains were rare and unpredictable and he had to bike twelve miles from the train station to reach our village. The village women also came to see the baby boy. They came in through the kitchen door with small presents of food for my mother. They kissed my mother four times; I had never seen them do that before. (I found out it was traditional in Normandy to kiss each cheek twice when women greeted one another. In Paris the tradition is only once.) My mother brought the baby to the kitchen. They admired him, they talked to him, they congratulated my mother.

"*Madame Atthalin, quel beau cadeau de Noel*," they said. "A son, you have a son, it's the best present, your Christmas present, just what you wanted, *un beau petit garçon.*" Even my schoolmistress came. She turned to me and said, "Now you have a baby brother." "But he is always sleeping," I said, disappointed. That was not the *Divin Messie* I had imagined. But he was making my mother happy. He was truly our little savior, saving us from our mother's discontent. So I was happy too. I enjoyed school even more, bundling up every morning, skipping down the hill, playing freely outdoors till dark with my friends in the cold damp fresh air.

And then came *les vacances de Noel,* our Christmas break, two weeks without school. And Christmas Day, *le jour de Noel,* arrived. We always celebrated Christmas Day the same way. We knew Jesus was born during the night. When we got up, we ran down to the dining room to look at the crèche. Yes, there was a tiny statue of a tiny baby in the manger; baby Jesus had come. We all stood in front of the crèche. My mother's baby was almost one month old and was sleeping in her arms, and baby Jesus was sleeping in his manger. We sang the Noel song:

Il est né le Divin Enfant,
Jouez Hautbois,
Résonnez Musettes
Il est né le Divin Enfant,
Chantons tous son Avènement.

(He is born, the Divine Child,
Play oboes,
And bagpipes
He is born, the Divine Child,
We all sing for his coming.)

I knew all the verses to this song as well. It was a very happy song.

Then we opened our presents and had cake and hot milk for breakfast, a traditional Christmas morning.

Nanny took my sisters back to their nursery to play with their new toys. My mother got busy with our cook planning the Noel dinner. She had invited our neighbors and needed to set the table. She asked me to hold the baby. She made me sit down where she always sat and placed him in my arms. She had never done that before.

The baby was sleeping in my arms, with his little body wrapped up and warm against my chest. I was rocking him gently, singing to him the Noel song, "*Il est né le Divin Enfant*," over and over again, very softly. I loved this song. There was a verse that sounded just like the baby:

Ah! qu'il est beau, qu'il est charmant,
Que ses grâces sont parfaites,
Ah! qu'il est beau, qu'il est charmant,
Qu'il est doux ce Divin Enfant.

(How lovely, how charming he is,
How gracious and perfect,

How lovely, how charming he is,
How sweet is this divine child.)

Sometimes I just hummed the tune, feeling happy to make my little music for the baby.

"It's like a lullaby," my mother said. "*Tu es une vraie petite maman*," she added.

Then I saw the baby open his eyes and look at me. I looked at him, he looked at me. It was the first time I saw his eyes wide open. He had big brown eyes. He was smiling. I thought he liked my song so I went on singing: "*Il est né le Divin Enfant.*" His little face was smiling all over. When I saw him smiling at me, I knew who he was. He was the one we had been waiting for, who makes everybody happy.

"You are my baby Jesus," I whispered to his tiny ear. "That's who you are, you are the *divin messie,* because you make everybody happy."

My parents had chosen the name Louis-Ferdinand for him. I asked my mother, "What kind of name is that?"

She explained, "Louis is the name of your father's great-grandfather, le Général Baron Louis Atthalin, aide-de-camp and intimate friend of King Louis-Philippe, and Ferdinand is the name of my grandfather, Ferdinand Foch, Maréchal de France. They are our great ancestors and we are proud of them. This is the right name for our first son."

All this did not mean much to me, but I understood more and more how important it was for my mother to have a son. None of us four girls had been named after any of our women ancestors. I guessed none of them were important

Odile, age five, in Paris before moving to Normandy

enough. As for me, I could never call my baby brother by such a weird name. Today, *le jour de Noel*, I knew what his name was. It was a secret, just between the two of us:

"*Tu es mon p'tit Jésus*," I repeated. He kept smiling and I knew his new name made him happy.

Chapter 2

Participation Mystique, Initiation to Spiritual Life at Age Seven

The baptism ritual at our little church was a few days later. Normally it's the godmother who holds the baby over the font, but since the chosen one, my mother's cousin, could not come from Paris, my mother made me hold the baby for his ceremony. I became his godmother for a moment, and I was very proud. When drops of water were poured on his forehead, he looked at me and smiled.

He was wearing a very beautiful embroidered long white dress handed down from my grandmother, which we had all worn before him. The people from the village, who all knew my mother, came and kissed her four times as usual, and admired her son. They saw me holding him. My schoolmistress said he looked like an angel.

I had another week of vacation and spent all my time watching Nanny caring for the baby. I learned to give the baby his bottle. My mother never nursed her children. I burped him, rocked him, and cuddled him. I also learned to bathe him, powder him, dress him, and stroke him.

When Nanny saw me caress his silky hair, she said, "*Tes petites mains sont la taille idéale pour son petit corps.*" (Your little hands are just the ideal size for his small body.)

Nanny would seat me on the low chair, place the baby almost naked on my lap and let me rub his back, his chest, and his tummy. I would play with his tiny toes, open his chubby fists, and kiss his lovely fingers. I would place my small hands on the sides of his head where they seemed to fit perfectly, and touch his face and ears, moving very slowly, very carefully, filled with love. He looked like he enjoyed it as much as I did. He was always watching my face. When he smiled, his whole face was smiling.

Whenever I was alone with him, I would talk to him, not baby talk like Nanny did, but real words: "*Tu es mon p'tit Jésus, un vrai de vrai, en chair et en os. C'est un secret. Tu me regardes et je sais que tu m'écoutes. Tu me regardes comme pour me dire que tu comprends tout.*" (You are my little Jesus, a real one, flesh and bones. It's a secret. You look at me, and I know you hear me, telling me that you understand everything.)

And: "*Quand je te tiens dans mes bras, je suis très heureuse. Quand je te serre contre moi, je sens mon coeur battre et même parfois j'ai des larmes dans mes yeux, pas des larmes de tristesse, mais des larmes de bonheur. Quand je suis à l'école, je pense à toi sans arrêt.*" (When I hold you, I am very happy. When I press you against me, I feel my heart beating, even sometimes I have tears in my eyes, not sad tears, but happy ones. When I am at school, I think of you all the time.)

I ran to him in the morning when I woke up. He immediately smiled when he heard my voice. In the evening before bed, I sang to him another Noel song I had learned at Catholic school:

Les anges dans nos campagnes
Ont entonné l'hymne des cieux
Et l'écho de nos montagnes
Redit ce chant mélodieux
Gloria . . . in excelsis deo.

(Angels in our countryside
Are singing the song of heaven
And the echo of our mountains
Repeat this melodious tune
Gloria . . . in excelsis deo.)

I would keep singing very softly the last line, "Gloria . . . Gloria . . . Gloria," until he closed his eyes and was asleep.

When I went back to school, I would run home at the end of the day, instead of playing with my school friends, to arrive in time for his evening bottle. My mother kept saying I was learning to be a mother and I was luckier than she had been, that she never had a younger sibling because her father died in the First World War soon after she was born. She never met her father and of course, her mother never had another child.

I was overjoyed to hold my little Jesus. He was not just another sibling. He was my baby, he was my best friend, he smiled at me, he looked at me, he made everyone happy. My sisters, although they were good little girls, could not make everybody happy.

My mother was getting restless. She had delivered a strong, healthy, beautiful baby boy. She had produced the perfect male infant; she had completed her number one assignment. She was done. Now she deserved a reward, and she was going to go and get it. She had been cooped up in a remote village for more than a year. She wanted to go to Paris, to celebrate the first son's birth with family and friends. Nanny was a trained professional nanny and she knew everything regarding babies. We also had Madame Coulon, our cook, who came from the village every morning, bringing bread and meat, and had become part of our little family. We had a housekeeper to clean the house, and another woman to do the laundry in the old-fashioned way, boiling the sheets, towels, diapers, and clothes in a huge boiler on a wood fire, in the little stone shed meant for this. And there was a gardener who kept a vegetable garden in the greenhouse. So my mother did not have much to do at home. Mostly she was out on her bicycle visiting the farmers, buying meat from them, packing it, and sending parcels to family and friends who were starving in Paris. She could leave us, assured that all our needs would be covered.

If trains ran, you never knew when you would arrive at your destination. And they could be bombed either by the *résistants* or the Germans, no one knew for sure. And of course there were no cars on the roads because there was no fuel. But it was not going to stop my mother. She decided she could bike the ten miles to Laigle, the nearest station, and just wait for the next train. She left very early on a foggy, cold winter morning with a small suitcase fastened to the rack of the bike. Her goodbyes to me included, "Take good care of your baby brother."

A few days later, I heard the baby crying at night, which was very unusual, as he had been a very easy, content baby. I got up and rushed to Nanny's room. When she picked him up, she found him very hot. His temperature was too high, she said. There was one doctor in the village and also a small pharmacy, but of course no phone. No one had a phone. The only phone was at the small grocery store at the center of the village about one mile from our house.

It was four in the morning, a very dark winter night. She said the baby was sick, and she must go to the village and bring the doctor back. She placed the baby in my arms. He stopped crying, and she hurried off.

"*Mon p'tit Jésus,*" I whispered, filled with my love, wishing to comfort him, but I noticed that he was not looking at me as he always did. He kept his eyes closed and soon fell asleep. So I kept quiet, listening for the front door to open, for footsteps coming up the stairs, for signs of Nanny returning with the doctor. All I heard was deep, thick silence inside and outside for a long time. I kept very still, holding my sleeping baby. And finally I must have fallen asleep too.

Next thing I knew Nanny was in the room, panting, alone, no doctor. She took the baby from my arms. She put her hand on his forehead, then pressed his small face against her ear, as if listening to him. Then she buried her face in his little chest. She was mumbling something to herself. All I could hear was "*trop tard, trop tard*" (too late, too late). The next minute, the pharmacist was rushing upstairs and Nanny said again, "*trop tard.*" He leaned over the baby's face, waited, and repeated "*trop tard*." I did not understand what they meant; they looked very serious.

What happened to the baby when we were both asleep together? Nanny said that he had gone to heaven, he had become an angel. She told me to go downstairs and wait for the cook, Madame Coulon, in the kitchen where it was warm. Madame Coulon soon arrived as she always did. She was surprised to find me in the kitchen, but I could not talk, I did not know what to say. Eventually Nanny came down and asked her to watch for my sisters when they woke up. She had to go to the village café that had the only telephone. She said it would be a long wait before she could be connected to my parents in Paris. She had to tell them what happened last night. She was very upset. I had never seen her like that. She turned to me:

"Don't let your sisters come into the baby's room."

"Can I go there?" I asked.

"Yes," she answered, "you can go, but don't touch him, don't disturb him, and keep your warm robe on, it's very cold in the room."

Madame Coulon gave me a bowl of hot milk. I went back upstairs to the baby's room. I was still in my pajamas and robe, woolen socks and slippers. No need to dress, I was not going to school today, just waiting for Nanny to return.

When I entered the room I had a strange feeling, a frisson, like a shiver of my whole body, the same feeling I had when I entered our village church but instead of being dark, the room was all white and filled with light. There was a white sheet draped on Nanny's bed. Outside the window the sky was very white too. The ground was covered with white frost. The baby was lying on top of his white blanket in his white christening gown. I quietly brought a chair right against his crib. I sat at the edge of the chair so that I could be as close to him as possible without touching him and kept my little hands on the rail of the crib. As I stared at him, I felt I could almost touch him with my eyes. His little face was so beautiful and so peaceful, it made me feel peaceful, too. I started talking to him. "Have you really become an angel?" I asked, and waited, but he did not open his eyes. I kept talking, thinking, maybe he will open his eyes later.

"I thought angels had wings and lived in the sky," I said. "Maybe that's what they call a mystery. I never saw a mystery before. Have you become a mystery? Is that why you can't open your eyes? Do angels keep their eyes closed?"

He had become my confidante. I never had a confidante before. I had a lot of secrets to tell him, so I kept talking.

"You are my little Jesus. I like sitting here with you even if you don't open your eyes. I know you love me just as I love you. I have never loved anyone like this before. You are the best friend of my heart. I adore you. Now I know what they mean when they sing, 'We adore you.' I will always adore you. This is our secret."

After a while, Madame Coulon came in and very softly told me to come downstairs for lunch. I leaned over to the baby's tiny ear and whispered, "*Je reviens tout de suite.*" (I will be back very soon.) All I wanted was to be with him, look at him, talk to him, and have him all to myself.

When Nanny came back from the village, her face was all red, as if she had cried the whole time she was gone. She said that my parents would arrive tomorrow afternoon. I wanted to spend more time with the baby, but Nanny wanted me to go to bed.

I woke up very early, four by the clock on the wall. Yesterday at this time the baby had been crying. Today the house was totally silent. I waited in bed, listening for Nanny to open her door, so I could go back to visit my baby as I did every morning before going to school.

Nanny let me in. Here he was. He had not moved. His tiny hands were still crossed together on his chest. His face was very white, as white as his beautiful dress. I sat by his side, adoring him again, until Nanny told me I must go and fetch our daily food from the farm. Nanny told me it was time to say goodbye to the baby, so I whispered, "*Au revoir, mon p'tit Jésus.*"

Nanny told me not to say anything to the farmer about the baby. "Just say that your mother is away, and Nanny is too busy to come to the farm today."

I went off with my empty basket and came back much later with the heavy milk jug in one hand and the bag of butter and cheese in the other hand. It was a long walk. The farmers were very friendly and gave me lunch with them, a thick soup and bread with a lot of butter.

When I got back, my parents had not arrived yet. We did not know how they would come from Paris. Would they find a train? How would they come from the station? Would they have to get a ride from a horse and buggy?

Nanny told me to wait downstairs. I sat by the dining room window and stared outside, listening for some sign of my parents' arrival.

I heard something far away, like a car driving up the road. It was coming closer and stopped at the front gate. I heard the huge iron gate grinding open on the gravel. I ran to the window of the sitting room facing the front yard. I saw Nanny rushing outside. I recognized the black Citroën of my wealthy grandfather, who still had a car because he was important.

I saw his chauffeur open the car doors. I saw four people, my parents and my grandparents, all dressed in black coats and black hats, come out of the car and walk to the front door with their heads down, following Nanny.

They went directly upstairs to Nanny's room, where the baby was lying in his crib. They did not see me on their way up. I did not follow them. They forgot about me.

I heard my mother screaming and crying very loudly for a long time. Then I heard my grandparents come downstairs and walk back to the car. The car drove out and the gate was closed again. I did not see my parents. Nanny said to be very good, very quiet, and not ask anything.

The next day, Nanny told me I had to go to school, I would see my parents later. When I arrived, my schoolmistress said to me, "*Ma petite Odile*, it's so sad," and she gave me a big hug, holding me against her big bosom. That made me cry. She said it was good to cry. She told me the baby had become my guardian angel, that he would love me and protect me for the rest of my life. She said that I could talk to him and he would talk back to me and if I was very quiet I would be able to hear him in my heart.

"But I can't hold him anymore," I mumbled.

When I got back home, I took my *boots* off in the kitchen as usual. I could not hear anyone or any noise in the house. So I tiptoed upstairs to see the baby. He was gone. The crib was gone. The room was empty. I went to the window and stared outside to the white clouds. Nanny found me in the room, still standing there, and said that my parents were out making arrangements. She said, "Tomorrow the baby will be buried."

He had disappeared, just like the *santons* and the crèche had disappeared at the end of the holidays. Between the Christmas Day when my mother gave me the baby to hold, and the last night I held him, it had been about two months. Mon p'tit Jésus had come for a visit and he had gone back to heaven. That's what I told myself. I thought, maybe he will come back, maybe next Christmas, maybe when the war is over. For now he was my guardian angel, he was still my best friend, and I could still talk to him. I spent a lot of time alone with him, keeping our secret.

My baby brother had opened a door in me to inner life, to devotion, to spirit, to mystery. His short life was my first time to love and be loved back, my first time talking about myself to anyone, my first time to have a secret self. It was all taken away so suddenly.

Chapter 3

Le Débarquement, D-day in Normandy, 1944

My mother was always mad, raving and ranting about the Germans. They had killed her father and all the men in her family during World War I, and now they had taken her only son, she said, because we had had to flee from Paris. There would have been a doctor in Paris and the baby would have been saved.

My mother would not talk to me anymore. I stayed out of her way. Nobody talked. Nanny kept my sisters very quiet. Madame Coulon kept cooking but did not talk. We ate in silence.

When I was not reading, I would sit in the dining room facing the big windows, and I gazed off into the sky. That irked my mother. "*Odile, tu rêvasses trop!*" she said. "*Fais quelque chose.*" (You're always daydreaming! Do something.)

At night when I was alone and quiet in bed, I would cross my arms tightly over my chest where I had held my baby brother, curl up my body, close my eyes, and whisper the name I had given him. I immediately felt a rush of warmth as if he were with me, right against my heart. I would repeat his special name, and fall asleep with this comforting feeling of my love for him. I kept telling him that I adored him, I would never lose him, that I would always love him, that was our secret. And it remained a secret to this very day, writing about it.

Soon it was springtime. I could spend more time by myself outdoors, lie in the meadows, and gaze at the sky as long as I wished. The swallows had returned. I watched them flying all around. They looked happy, and my heart flew with them.

On June 6, 1944, things changed dramatically. Very early in the morning—it was still dark—my mother woke me up, shouting: "Wake up, they are coming, c'est le débarquement. Listen . . . can you hear?"

Yes, we heard very loud noises coming from the beach where we went during the summer. "The cannons on the coast!" my mother exclaimed. And loud noises in the sky: squadrons passing over our heads, fighter planes zipping all over, while my mother was screaming, "Les alliés ont débarqué! Les alliés ont débarqué!" (The allied forces have arrived!)

We were rushed to the trench that had been dug behind the house down the hill, away from the road, safe, we hoped, from planes and tanks. We stayed there with Nanny, while my mother went back and forth to the house and brought back what we needed to eat and sleep. After three days, it was safe to get out. The Americans had arrived. Everybody ran out to greet them. We saw American jeeps and tanks rolling through our village. Some people laughed and screamed with joy, some cried and sobbed. Some climbed onto the tanks to hug the soldiers. Everyone hugged everyone, including us children who passed from one embrace to another. The soldiers threw cans of food, cigarettes, and candies—the first candies we ever had—to whomever could catch them. That's when my mother came back to life.

We moved back to Paris. I saw the Liberation parade, from the balcony on the fifth floor of our friends' apartment building. I saw huge crowds waving millions of French flags, and our new leader, General de Gaulle, tall, tough, proud, marching down the Champs Elysees with the victorious army. Three days later, I saw the Franco-American military parade and the popular exultation of one and all, especially of my mother, who kept screaming with pride and vengeance.

I never went back to the Normandy house where we had spent the occupation and D-day. I kept the memories of our last winter tucked away all to myself in my heart.

Life had taken such a different turn there was no more time for daydreaming, nor for gazing off, no quiet time, no solitude, no room for sadness. That's when people started asking me: "Odile, why do you always look sad even when you smile?" And they would add, "*avec ton sourire de Joconde*" (with your Mona Lisa smile). This Joconde person meant nothing to me, but from the tone of their voices, I understood it was not a compliment.

Chapter 4

Dr. Rosen, My First Healing Experience

*"There is no agony like bearing an untold story
inside of you."—Maya Angelou*

The first summer after the war, we went back to Normandy, not to the house where we had spent the Occupation, but to the old family mansion, "Le Château." The Germans had ruined most of the inside. The floors and the walls had been wrecked and the French doors had been broken, but a lot of remodeling and cleaning up had made it possible for the whole family to gather again.

The gathering included my paternal grandparents and their four married children with their nineteen grandchildren, plus four nannies, cooks, servants, a chauffeur, and so on. Downstairs were the kitchens, the pantries, the huge dining room, two large living rooms, and two private drawing rooms, one for each of the grandparents, a big lobby, a verandah on one side, and a terrace on the other. The bedrooms were upstairs, three floors of bedrooms, the first floor for the adults, the second floor for the children and their respective nannies, and the third floor for the domestics, the typical feudal organization.

My sisters and I shared a large room with four beds, and our cousins shared the other bedrooms on the same floor.

In the middle of the summer, I started complaining of chest pain. So far I had been a very healthy child, strong, smart, studious, and considered mature for my age.

My mother made me take some deep breaths to check if it hurt more when I did. Yes, it did hurt a lot more. I kept my breathing as shallow as possible to avoid the sharp pain. It felt like something was tearing inside my chest.

When the adults heard of my condition, they panicked. One of my cousins, the same age as I was, who had experienced similar chest pain, had died of tuberculosis the previous year. Here again was the deadly TB bacteria, ready to take another life.

"*Le bacille de Koch*," they repeated, and I could hear the dread in their voices. In the forties, TB was a fatal disease. Coughing, sneezing, even speaking, and of course breathing could spread it. The "*bacille de Koch*" was the culprit. It was in my body, and that made me the culprit, too. The punishment followed: I was removed from the bedroom I shared with my three sisters, and isolated in a tiny room on the third floor where nobody was allowed to visit. Quarantined, except for the doctor.

Dr. Rosen lived in Laigle, about twenty miles away, and was called to see me. I remember the first time he came to my solitary room. I was in bed with low fever and chest pain.

He sat next to my bed, looked into my eyes, touched my hand, and smiled, as if he was happy to see me and had nothing better to do. I had plenty of time to look at him. His face was darker than those of the people I knew. He had black eyes, short black curly hair, and long golden fingers resting on my hand. His smile was full of very white teeth. I liked him right away and took a deep breath of relief.

"*Ay*," I exclaimed, "*ça fait mal.*" (Ouch, that hurt.) I said, "it hurts when I breathe."

"Yes," replied Dr. Rosen, "could you show me where it hurts?"

"Here," I said, and showed him with my hand on the left side of my chest, on top of my nightdress.

"May I put my hand there, too?" he asked gently. "Could you guide my hand to where it hurts?"

My fingers on top of his hand, I could feel how soft his skin was. He kept his hand on my pain for a long time without saying anything. He was looking at me. I was looking at him. I felt I was going to cry.

"Is my hand hurting you?" he asked me.

"*Oh non, ça me fait du bien*," I replied. (It feels good.) "Your hand feels good on my side."

"Then it's OK if I keep my hand here a little longer?" he asked. "I am listening to your breathing."

With his big hand on my small chest listening to me, I could let myself breathe a little more.

Eventually Dr. Rosen pulled out his stethoscope and told me he needed to listen deeper inside my chest.

Before he left, he told me he would come back tomorrow. He came back every day. He sat next to me the same way, placed his right hand on my left chest, stayed put, and talked to me.

After he got the blood tests, Dr. Rosen diagnosed that

it was not the "*bacille de Koch*" hurting my lung. He told me it was an inflammation of the pleura.

"The pleura," he explained, "is the lining around the lung. The pleura around your left lung is inflamed and rubs against your lung and it hurts every time you breathe in. It's a disease called pleurisy."

"*Pleurésie*," I echoed. "It sounds like *pleurer* (to weep). It reminds me of a poem of Verlaine: *Il pleure dans mon coeur* (It weeps in my heart). I learned it by heart at school. Dr. Rosen, don't you think it sounds like *pleurer*?"

"Yes, it does sound like *pleurer*. It is as if your lung is weeping," he said. "When you look at me, I see a brave little girl who is lonely and very sad."

I felt shy and closed my eyes. Tears rolled down my cheeks. They spoke for me.

"Sadness is a good thing," Dr. Rosen told me. "I have been very sad myself for many years. I wept very often during the war, I was so lonely," he shared.

"Why were you sad?" I wanted to know why this wonderful man could be so lonely.

"It's a long story, maybe I will tell you when you feel better," said Dr. Rosen.

"I already feel better, will you tell me your story?" I pleaded.

"Yes," he assured me, "I will, tomorrow."

The family calmed down when they heard of the diagnosis, but they kept me quarantined just in case.

Sometimes my mother would come to see me for a few minutes. I asked her why Dr. Rosen looked so different.

"He is Jewish," she explained. And she added: "He is the best doctor around, and he comes every day all the way from Laigle to see you, so he is a really good doctor."

Dr. Rosen had been a well-known and well-loved family physician for several years before the war. His wife and daughter would often go to Paris to visit his wife's Jewish family for a few days. The last time they went to Paris, they never came back. They were caught, all three generations, grandparents, mother, and daughter, in one of the earliest Nazi round-ups.

Dr. Rosen had to hide immediately. A devoted nurse provided a secret space in her family's home cellar. At the end of the war, he learned the dreaded truth. He returned to his medical practice, the only thing left to him.

Dr. Rosen, as he had promised, told me about his sadness.

"The last time I saw my daughter, it was on the platform of the train station, in Laigle, waiting for the train to Paris," he said. "She was happy. It was summer, she was six years old, she wore a white dress and had long black curly hair. She was so pretty and so excited, running and dancing up and down the platform, jumping on me, hugging me and kissing me. I was very anxious about seeing them go off, but she kept saying, 'Don't worry, Papa, we will be back Wednesday and we'll bring you a surprise.' She would be eight years old now, just like you," he said, looking at me with his sad smile.

We kept silent; my heart was too full to speak. I liked Dr. Rosen so much I wished I could be his daughter and hug him and make him happy again.

I must have sighed too deeply because I had a sudden sharp pain in my chest. "Ay!" I cried. Dr. Rosen put his hand on the pain. I felt relieved and closed my eyes.

What will happen when I am not sick anymore? I wondered. When we go back to Paris, will I ever see Dr. Rosen again? Will I lose him and be lonely all over again?

"Dr. Rosen, are you lonely?" I asked.

"I was very lonely for two years," he replied, "when I was stuck in my cave. I wanted to go out and look for them. At times, my host had to lock me in to make sure I would not go outside. It would have been too dangerous. There was nothing I could do for them. Yes, I felt very lonely."

"And now?" I kept asking.

"Now it's different. I miss them. I will always miss them. I look at them, at a beautiful picture of them together, on the mantelpiece in my bedroom. They are smiling at me, and I smile back. I feel so much love for them, it's as if we are still together in a way."

"In what way?" I insisted.

"In my heart, in the love we felt for each other. Our souls will always be together," he explained.

The more Dr. Rosen talked, the more I wanted him to continue. I also felt lonely, in my tiny bedroom with my books, not knowing how long it would be before I could get out. Dr. Rosen knew how I felt.

I kept asking questions. "What are souls?"

He paused, took his time and said, "Well, right now your body is sick, your lung hurts, you are in pain, but another part of you feels safe and loved and peaceful. Well, that part of you is your soul. You are feeling your soul when you feel that you love someone. Your soul never gets sick and never dies. You can love people even when they are dead. Your soul and their soul continue to love each other."

It was so soothing to listen to him I wanted to keep my eyes closed, not move, and just feel his hand on mine. After a while, Dr. Rosen got up. "Sweet dreams, I will see you tomorrow," he said.

The next day, as soon as Dr. Rosen had settled on his chair next to me, I asked him, "Dr. Rosen, would you tell me about your daughter again?"

But this time, he was the one who had a question. "How about you telling me about your baby brother?"

I got scared. How did Dr. Rosen know? I felt the pain in my chest get sharper and I cringed, pulling back into my pillow. I put my head down. I could not look at him and mumbled very fast, "They said he died when we were both sleeping together, before Nanny came back."

Dr. Rosen leaned toward me and asked very gently, "Were you holding him?"

"Yes," I whispered with my head down.

"Could you show me how you were holding him?" he asked, putting his hand on my crouching shoulders.

"Just in my arms like that," I showed him, putting my arms together like a cradle. "I thought he was sleeping," I added, trembling.

"I see," said Dr. Rosen, watching me and speaking slowly. "You were holding him in your arms and hugging him against your heart and cradling him and he fell asleep

. . . You kept holding him and he kept sleeping . . . He was quiet and cozy in your arms, against your heart full of love for him."

Then Dr. Rosen stopped and tenderly added, "And in his sleep his soul left his body."

I looked up. Dr. Rosen, a tear rolling down his cheek, was smiling at me. I knew he understood. I felt safe again and wanted him to keep talking to me.

"Where did his soul go?" I asked.

"All we know is that it's important to be held in loving arms when the soul leaves the body . . . so that the soul feels loved when it leaves . . . This is what you gave to your baby brother, your loving arms, that was your gift to him . . . We know that when the soul leaves the body peacefully, like he did, the soul goes on a beautiful journey."

I felt a rush of tears inside of me. I could not hold them back any more. They overflowed and I broke down. Dr. Rosen kept holding my hand with both hands, and told me it was good to cry, that crying would heal my lung.

After the death of my baby brother, I was too afraid of my mother to ask questions, of making her mad, so I became silent. Nobody had talked to me. I walked around with an open heart and no one to love. People around me were too busy, too taken by the huge changes the country was going through, too excited to pay attention to the feelings of a lonely little girl. My open heart went underground.

Then Dr. Rosen came into my life. He was so different. He talked about love. He spoke slowly and softly, he was calm and sweet, his hands were safe and loving—all qualities that were missing in my family. He listened to me, he understood my disease and its cause, he was not worried, he talked to me, he asked me questions, and he explained to me how I felt. He healed my weeping lung and my loneliness. He put the seed of meditation in me, showing me how to feel and know myself. He put me on the path to "an examined life," the only one worth living.

Chapter 5

My Personal Odyssey, Years of Searching Around the World

"I am open to the guidance of synchronicity, and
do not let expectations hinder my path."
—*14th Dalai Lama*

At the end of the summer, my lungs were considered too fragile to breathe the polluted urban air of Paris. I was sent to a boarding school in the country, a beautiful place surrounded by trees, woods, and vegetable farms, about two hours from Paris by train.

My caretakers and teachers were nuns. They were devoted to us and gave us the best education, but they did not pay attention to how we felt. I missed Dr. Rosen too much and had to forget about him. For my family, Dr. Rosen was the local doctor, and when he was not needed anymore, he was forgotten.

For me, the separation had been too brutal. Dr. Rosen had appeared, had given a new dimension to my life, sowing new seeds for a spiritual life, and had disappeared. I had to put away my relationship with him in some treasure chest, like a diamond ring too precious to wear every day, kept in a safe and never taken out, until one forgets about it and even loses the key to the chest. Maybe it was in the same treasure chest where the short-lived great love for my baby brother got put away too. I had had a spiritual experience with the baby and then a healing experience with my doctor, but there was no room for a seeking heart in my daily life.

Boarding school was a haven after all the crises undergone: the bombings in Paris, the exodus, the years of occupation, the constant anguish expressed by the adults, the loss of the baby, the end of the war, my disease, and the healing experience.

But I felt different from my peers, as if my train had switched to a different track, and I was going to some unknown place on my own. I did not know how to have fun, how to giggle with the girls, how to be part of them.

I was a studious and excellent pupil in all fields, even gym. Learning and pleasing my teachers was my refuge. But deep down, I was asking myself lots of questions: What was my calling? What did my destiny have in store for me? Where did I belong? Who was going to guide me? I knew intuitively that my fate was not the traditional life marked out for me in my patriarchal bourgeois family. I did not want to be my mother all over, trapped, nor did I want to be a nun, also trapped. What other options were there? One path was to be a student and seeker. That's when my spiritual quest started.

One of my boarding school years was special. In order to become fluent in English I was sent to a boarding school in England, a big adventure for me at age thirteen. I traveled by myself, by train, and then onto the ship to cross the channel, and then another train. I tasted independence and loved it. I felt my potential. I felt more alive away from "them," my parental figures, and I knew that one day I would leave Paris. It was just a matter of time. I yearned for adventures, for travels, running away and cutting loose.

The mother superior, who had a loving eye on me, told me when I was fifteen and I finally left the convent, "Only service will fulfill you."

Five years later, when I was at the Sorbonne majoring in comparative literature, I heard about the Fulbright Foreign Student Program offered by the US government. I applied, although one had no idea what university one would be assigned to, in the whole fifty American states. I was ready to go anywhere. I was twenty, and the call to adventure was resounding loud and clear. When I heard I was going to New York City, I was thrilled.

When the grand ocean liner, the RMS Queen Elizabeth, after six days at sea passed the Statue of Liberty at sunrise and slowly glided into Manhattan harbor, I was on deck and felt my whole being, body and mind, expanding. A few hours later, I found myself on the Columbia University campus, having received a full scholarship from Barnard College and having been accepted as a junior in the American literature and drama departments.

I discovered a multicultural world, got into acting on campus, went to acting school in the Village, became a beatnik, smoked pot, and had plenty of love and sex during four years that confirmed my need for freedom, and also my recognition that Americans, after saving our country and being so generous to me, offered a more open society.

Four years later, after my student visa was over, I was back in Paris and was handed a book, *Life Against Death*, by Norman O. Brown, which showed me the next step: to learn about the unconscious. Maybe I would discover what I was looking for. Maybe I would find out who I was. Maybe I would uncover the secret meaning of my life. And it was with great expectations that I went back to school at the University of Montpellier, and got into the psychology program, to eventually become a psychoanalyst. So far I had explored the outer world of education, relationships, travels. Now I was turning to the inner world through introspection, and analysis of my shadow. But I was disappointed. I had been looking for role models and had found only impersonal scholars. After four years, I dropped out of academia, leaving an unfinished PhD.

At that time I had a horrible abortion. In those days of sexual liberation, before the eruption of AIDS, we had plenty of opportunities and partners. I had tried contraceptives, including the pill, but I had an aversion to them all and had given them up. I had heard of a condition that ran in my family. One of my first cousins who tried to get pregnant found out that her fallopian tubes were blocked. In order to have her three kids, she had to have her tubes surgically opened each time.

Blocked tubes, I thought, that is the best contraceptive

possible. What a gift of nature! Maybe my tubes are blocked too. What a relief that would be, never touching a contraceptive again, never to worry anymore!

I decided to get examined at the local hospital. Yes, my tubes were clogged, both of them, was the gynecologist's diagnosis. Good news, I was free!

But about two months later I found out I was pregnant. The incompetent internist had opened my tubes inadvertently and had not informed me, or probably did not even notice. I could have killed him. Instead I was going to kill the fetus.

My best friend kept nagging me: "Have you considered for a moment, just for a moment, having this baby?"

"No, I will never consider it, not even for a moment," was my response.

"Why, what does it mean to you?"

"A medical mistake! A child spermed by that crazy destructive drunk, no, never! I need to get rid of that man too. No, I will never give in."

"You might be losing an opportunity, maybe you will never be able to have children again, you are already thirty," she kept insisting.

"I never wanted to have children," I threw back at her, "and I never will. I have no desire to be a mother. I am independent and will remain independent." She gave up.

After all, I was an intellectual, empowered by one of my role models, Simone de Beauvoir, to reject any kind of domestication.

Abortion was still illegal. It took me another month to find the midwife known in the students' underground world. By the time the fetus was finally aborted, it was almost three months old. I never talked about it and pretended it had never happened.

But those three months shook me up. I had to question everything about my lifestyle, my sexuality, my relationships, my studies, and my purpose. My partner was a drunk and I was becoming one myself. There was a sense of absence and emptiness in my life. Something big was missing.

What followed the abortion was a radical change for the better. I turned my life around. I left my partner. I dropped out of my PhD studies. I ended my personal psychoanalysis for good. I turned on, tuned in, and moved on.

I moved to the magic island of Formentera, Spain, which had suddenly become a haven for American hippies who gave away free LSD. During my first ecstatic trip, dropping deeper into my inner world, I heard an inner voice telling me, "Go to India, go to India, Mother India, a pilgrimage back to the source." My elder friend and LSD guide, Margarita, who had been a follower of Krishnamurti and had attended his retreats in India for years, arranged for me to be the guest of her Bombay friend whenever I arrived.

I traveled overland by myself. First by train from Paris to Venice, where I got on a ship to Beirut and was greeted by a family acquaintance. From Lebanon, I took a bus to Damascus, Syria, and another bus to Baghdad, to arrive in Tehran, where I had a connection at the French consulate. I traveled with a Franco-Iranian medical group, which was establishing a leper colony at the easternmost border of Iran and Afghanistan. And from there, I took another bus to reach Kabul, where I met Farid, an Afghani who had been a student and close friend in France, and who showed me his country for several weeks. From Afghanistan, I went off with three friends to visit the high valleys of Kashmir in Pakistan, and lived with a Sufi family for two months. After all these detours and adventures, to finally reach Bombay, I got on a plane and arrived on this most memorable full moon night of May 1971.

During my first weeks in Bombay the focus of my life changed radically. After meeting several spiritual teachers, I understood why I had come to India. Eventually I was encouraged to visit an ashram in a remote country village. This was where I had my first experience of the yoga of meditation, which was going to change my life for good.

It happened on my very first day at the ashram. After meeting the spiritual teacher, I was taken to the meditation cave, and found myself going down a steep flight of steps to a small empty room, dark except for the light of a small candle. The assistant showed me where to sit on the carpeted floor, then walked out and closed the door.

I could not stay seated long. My body was suddenly seized with intense uncontrollable shaking. I started rolling all over the floor, my limbs stretching in all directions, my head flinging violently. I was a volcano erupting. Energy exploding inside me was spreading, pouring, racing through my body like lava. I was sobbing for no reason. My face was going through contortions, my mouth opening wider and wider, my eyes drawing in, then popping out. It felt like my body was a prison and an irresistible force was pressing and pushing from inside against the walls of the prison. I was gasping for more breath, breathing fire in and out like a dragon, and at the same time feeling totally safe, even exhilarated.

After a while, how long I could not know, feeling bodiless, emotionless, egoless, mindless, weightless, I remained flat on the floor in a state of perfect peace and a bliss I had never known.

This was the kind of direct experience and breakthrough I had been craving. When I was a teenager, I had read a line from the great French poet Rimbaud that had stuck with me like a mantra: "*O que ma quille éclate! O que j'aille à la mer!*" It was a line from a poem titled "The Drunken Boat," meaning: "O if only my keel would explode! O if only I could merge with the ocean!"

I had always felt confined, restricted, stifled, oppressed. I had been striving to free myself with sex, drugs, and rock and roll, and even psychoanalysis, all in vain.

This time, a new being and a new sense of who I was had emerged. It felt very simple, like the most natural state, of innocence, of total ease, of pure contentment and blissful connection to everything around me, a state of love and oneness with all. I remained in this state for ten days.

I was told later that this was a kundalini awakening. According to the Yogic tradition, within all of us dwells a spiritual energy, or Shakti, which resides at the base of the spine in a potential state. When awakened, kundalini

Shakti guides our transformation toward greater awareness and the bliss of pure love.

After ten days I lost this inner paradise. The purpose of meditation, I learned, was to keep reclaiming this blissful state as my true nature. I could return to it again and again. I became a passionate meditator.

I stayed in the ashram for the next three years, following the strict, relentless daily schedule from four A.M. till nine P.M. I studied all aspects of yoga (hatha, bhakti, kundalini, karma, jnana, raja) and the ancient scriptures related to the spiritual traditions of Vedanta, Sivaism, and Tantrism.

I saw how my habits to resist, to rebel, to judge, to close myself off, and to separate myself, which had helped me survive so far, were at this point a dead end and the source of my suffering. To relax the grip of the ego was the work of the awakened Shakti. Everyone in the ashram was going through her or his own process, knowing that it was all the Shakti's inner works of purification.

The hours of chanting, accompanied by the tablas, tamboura, and cymbals, were powerful. We had five one-hour sessions of chanting every day, during which I could pour my wounded heart out. From the dry intellectual I had been, I was transforming into a heart being, a devotional being. I loved this new tender self and knew it was my real self, the one I had experienced when I was in love with my baby brother at seven. Here was my life lesson, to keep opening my heart, whatever happened on the outside, not just during the chanting hours, to choose love over and over again, to reach out to love beyond fear, to give love, receive love, let love flow.

When I had been in the ashram for three years, a group of us disciples traveled with our teacher, who was opening meditation centers around the world, from India to Australia, to Hawaii, to California, to New York, to Paris. It was time to practice on the road and in the world what we had absorbed within the support of the ashram, to practice meditation and love for all in selfless service, in service to a higher cause.

As part of the staff, I served in different capacities, from dishwasher to translator, from cook to public relations person, to monitor, and counselor for new people who had just experienced a kundalini awakening.

We spent one year at the new ashram in Oakland, California, where I heard of the new forms of psycho-spiritual body-oriented therapies and made significant personal connections. I knew this was where I would eventually come back to.

At the end of the tour back to Paris, I met and became the student of a wandering Sufi teacher who taught a meditation practice, based on very slow gentle heart-focused movements and dances, saturated with ancient spiritual music. The goal was the same, to follow the creative Shakti, my inner life force, to purify and harmonize my whole being. This was exactly what I needed. The unfolding of the inner Shakti had manifested as kriyas, intense spontaneous movements experienced during meditation and chanting sessions, and had awakened in me a passionate dancer. I

Odile, transformed into a dancer

kept attending these Sufi meditation retreats for the next
three years, in New York State, Colorado and New Mexico.

Finally, after accumulating so many experiences that
showed me who I was and what my calling was, I needed
to reclaim my professional life. I had become a permanent
resident of the USA in 1979. I knew the Bay Area was where
I was going to find what I was looking for. I wanted to work
with body/mind/spirit all in one as a bodywork therapist,
and as a self-awareness teacher through yoga, movement
and dance forms of meditation, bringing together all the
trainings I had experienced and internalized.

In 1982, I got into my old Toyota station wagon and headed for California, lingering through the deserts and canyons of New Mexico and Arizona, spending starry nights on the cozy futon at the back of my car, slowly saying goodbye to the lands of enchantment and the life of the wandering dervish.

I felt assured that through meditation I could always reconnect with my awakened inner self, that deeper part of me, the source of peace, love, and bliss, which I had experienced so powerfully. Meditation had become a way of life.

Chapter 6

My Mother's Death, Paris 1986

May 1986. I had settled in Berkeley, California. The day after I celebrated my fiftieth birthday with my new friends, my sister Thérèse, an MD, who had always lived in Paris with her husband, also an MD, and their three children, called me. Thérèse told me: "If you wish to see your mother one more time, you better get on a plane now." I did not hesitate, and I was in Paris four days later.

My mother had her own large bedroom overlooking a quiet courtyard. The apartment was in an elegant art deco building on the rue Vavin in Paris. Mother and Father had lived in separate bedrooms for years, in this flat where they had moved after their six children had gone.

Her comfortable single bed stood in the center of the room like a throne, surrounded by shining antique mahogany furniture. The curtains and armchair covers were of a rich, cherry-pink damask satin.

Outside the large window the sky was filled with the *marronnier* (horse chestnut tree), an extraordinary presence. The huge tree rose from its roots in the backyard, and stretched its exuberant branches like arms reaching into my mother's fourth-floor bedroom window.

On the walls to the right and the left of this special window were two revealing portraits. One was a large sepia photograph of my mother at age ten, a child with deeply-set dark eyes and two long, very thick dark braids falling on her chest down to her waist. She was standing next to her commanding grandfather, Marshal Ferdinand Foch, the prestigious French military leader who had been supreme commander of the Allied forces at the end of World War I and who had remained in the popular mind as "the winner of the war." In the photo, he stood tall and straight although he was in his eighties, wearing a three-piece suit, a stiff white high collar and large tie with pin, a thick mustache, and a felt fedora. They were standing side by side, attentive to the photographer. My mother, Anne Bécourt-Foch, shy yet beautiful and proud, was leaning slightly toward him. He exuded total mastery and elegance, and although he had a cane, he was not leaning on it. Both had the same delicate smile and looked as if they could stand there forever.

Foch was the only adult male left in the whole extended family after World War I. My mother's father and uncles had all been killed at the front. So Bon-Papa, as she called him, was the father figure for two generations of widows and orphans. She lived in his glorified shadow long after he died in 1929. He filled her with a sense of identity and worth. He was still there for her in this picture, setting an impossible standard for other men.

The other portrait was an oil painting of me at age twenty-two, when I was a student in New York City. I gave it to my mother later on, when I dropped out and left for India for an indefinite time.

For the next twenty years, this portrait was all my mother had of her lost daughter, who was determined to not become a dissatisfied wife and a pregnant mother delivering a baby every year. The painting showed me dressed as a Mexican peasant (although I had not been to Mexico yet) wearing a bright multicolored poncho, with long black hair pulled back. I imagined my mother looking at the portrait, thinking: "This is my first child. She is looking away. She has betrayed her class; she has moved to distant lands and does not write letters. I don't blame her."

After years of this virtual presence, I had become a myth, now perceived as a contemplative, almost a saint, living in an ashram. This thought comforted my mother. The last postcard I received from her the year before she died represented a statue of the Black Madonna, an ancient, mysterious image of Mary, that she had found visiting an old French country church. My mother wrote: "*Je regarde cette image de la Madone et je te retrouve, tu as toujours eu la même expression de détachement que je vois aussi sur ton portrait dans ma chambre, différente de mes autres filles.*" (I look at this picture of the Madonna and I see you as I have always seen you, you always had the same look of detachment, just the way you look on your portrait in my room, different from my other daughters.) I had become a Black Madonna for my mother.

It was in this room that I came to my mother from Berkeley many years later and spent several weeks watching over her as she prepared to die.

After three extremely grueling chemotherapies at the hospital, the doctors had to admit that nothing more could be done for her besides pain management, and my mother had come home. She was getting close to the end.

When I showed up, my mother greeted me with a smile

of wonder and adoration, as if the Madonna had come to her, to ease her pain and shower her with love. And this is who I became. I was ready then, after ashram training in meditation, devotion, and surrender, to become the one my mother needed me to be as she was transitioning. As Maya Angelou once said, at age fifty each of us has become the person we always wanted to be. I realized this was true for me.

Although it was painful to watch my mother suffer, I could not leave her room, nor could I take my eyes off her as she lay in her bed. At times she would tell me to go out for a walk. I would arrive at the Luxembourg Garden, just a block away. It was summertime; I would linger under the thick, shading trees and by the pretty flower arrangements, but after a few minutes, I realized I missed my mother and soon would walk back and sit by her side again. I was falling in love with my mother.

My mother and I bonded for the first time. She was seventy-two; I was fifty. It started when I needed to take her in my arms. She hated the idea of peeing in a bedpan. Although her legs were too weak, she wanted to go to the bathroom. I would walk her there, almost carrying her.

Soon she needed to have a pee chair set next to her bed. I would help her sit up, rotate her body, put her feet on the floor, seat her on the pee chair and keep her from falling forward. And then take her back to bed. I would put my arms under her arms, enfold her, press her against my chest and absorb all her weight. That was a lot of holding and hugging. Her body was emaciated, nothing but skin and bones. I was deeply moved by our contact. It was nothing like cuddling: that would have been too intimate for us. But I felt I was embracing her as a most fragile treasure, with respect and love. I was grateful for this chance to be close to my mother, grateful that I had to repeat these motions over and over again. I was taking it in, feeling how healing it was for both of us.

Although my mother did not say so, I knew it was the same for her. She would not let anyone else move her. If the visiting nurse, or one of my siblings, would try to help her, she would ask in her weakening voice: *"Non, non, appelle Odile."* (No, no, call Odile.) No one else could touch her.

I did not want to miss any of it. This was what we never had, my mother and I, and certainly what she never had from her own mother. The negative feelings I had toward my mother, my resentment, my judgments, my desertion, were all gone. She had changed so much. She had become vulnerable and receptive, as opposed to impatient and peremptory. And I had changed too. I became the mother I never had, and the mother she never had either.

She said rare words of appreciation such as she had never said to me before. It was about my voice. I had been reading to her beautiful spiritual texts like some of the Psalms. Her weak but loving words were, *"Quelle belle voix!* You read so well, you have such a lovely voice. I love listening to you. Continue, keep reading."

Her bitterness had fallen away. What was left was her unique essence, her innocence. She had finally allowed one of her five daughters into her heart, her first child, who had abandoned her but had returned.

Toward the end, she could only mumble: *"C'est trop long, trop long, j'en ai assez."* (It's taking too long, too long, I have had enough.)

We were not quite done. Our body contacts had brought us together, but that was not enough. I needed to say the words that would bring our relationship to its completion. During the thirty years I had been away, we had followed our separate and diverging paths, but they had brought us back to one another, here in this room for a short time, before we parted again. We never mentioned our past estrangement; there was no need for it. I spoke slowly, distinctly, precisely.

"You gave me the most precious gift when I was born," I told her. "You gave me your life and my life. You gave me good genes and good health. You gave me my independence and my freedom." I took a deep breath. "Now you are giving me another great gift." I paused. "I am reading these divine texts to you. This time together is special, I love your sweetness, your courage, your peace." I paused again. "I have fallen in love with your spirit. You are giving me a great example." Pause. "For me this is the supreme teaching, how to be at the end of life, how to go through this great mystery, the passage into the next world. You are giving a boost to my spiritual life." Pause. "Yes," I repeated, "you gave me a good physical life and now you are giving me a renewed spiritual life. *Merci infiniment.*"

My mother kept her eyes closed. Then in her tiny voice she said, *"C'est mon plus grand plaisir."* (It's my greatest pleasure.)

A few hours later, she went into a coma. These were her last words.

*Black Madonna, Puy-de-Dome,
France*

My mother died content, I told myself. That was her last gift
to me. My mother died on July 3, 1986.

Several days after the funeral, since I had to remain
in Paris a little longer, it was suggested that I move into
my mother's bedroom. In her bed I slept the most peaceful
nights, the large window open to let in the summer warmth.
Turning my head slightly to the left, I would get lost in the
dense green foliage of the *marronier,* our living witness,
and I would repeat to myself my mother's last words: "*C'est
mon plus grand plaisir . . . c'est mon plus grand plaisir.*"

It was less than a year later that Gaby was born, on May 3,
1987.

Chapter 7

Meeting Newborn Gaby;
Berkeley for Good

"There is but one salvation for the tired soul:
love for another person. For what is love, but the
lover makes the soul of his beloved his sphere
and they are one in spirit."
—José Ortega y Gasset

I met Gaby before he was born.

It took an amazing series of circumstances for me to arrive in Berkeley, find a home, make the right professional connections, focus on my work as a body-mind therapist and yoga instructor, and be ready, available, and fully present for this event.

Rena, a psychotherapist and close friend, who had attended my yoga classes, had invited me for a Seder dinner at her home. I remember this crucial evening in every detail. This was April 14, 1987. I arrived early and was warmly welcomed. As I walked in, I saw a very long table covered with a white tablecloth, fully set and decorated for the event with flowers, wine bottles, and elegant glasses, a festive sight:

"What a beautiful table," I admired.

"This is the largest seder I have ever had in my home. Twenty people are coming," Rena confirmed.

Watching the guests arrive, I noticed a glamorous woman walk in: she was in her thirties, with a lovely, classical face, well made-up, wearing a long, silky, salmon-colored shirt covering a very pregnant belly, no doubt in the fullness of her time, looking confident and in charge. Together with her were a man, also in his thirties, and a young child. Rena stepped in and introduced us: Odile Atthalin, Nicole Liboiron; Jeremy Cohen, the husband; and Zachary, their three-year-old son. She added, pointing to me, "Nicole, this is the woman I told you about."

Nicole, perfectly bilingual, immediately started to speak French to me. Nicole was from Montreal, Quebec. She was more than eight months pregnant, she said, holding her big belly. She needed help, and Rena had recommended me as a body-mind therapist.

"Could you give me some bodywork treatments?" Nicole asked.

"Of course," I said, without hesitation.

"I don't have a car. Could you come to my home?" she asked.

"Of course," I repeated.

"The sooner the better!" Nicole added.

"Of course," I continued, understanding the urgency and pulling out my card. Then I inquired about the baby.

"Yes, it's a boy," Nicole said.

"Do you have a name for him?" I asked.

"I am not sure. I want a name that sounds good in French and in English."

"Like Gabriel?" I heard myself suggest, to my own surprise.

"Yes, exactly, that's what I was thinking: Gabriel. We could call him Gaby, I love the sound of Gaby," she added.

And that's how I met Gaby before he was born. He was still in the womb but he was already very present.

We all sat down for the Seder dinner. Nicole was at one end of the long table, taking care of her three-year-old son. As the ritual proceeded, I realized I was in an altered state, staring into the distance, questioning what had just happened to me. The way I said yes to Nicole without thinking, as if moved by some alien force. And how about the naming of the baby, Gabriel, and the synchronicity of our choices, Gabriel, the angel messenger? Why did this name pop out of me so eagerly?

Famous images of the archangel appearing to Mary passed on my mental screen. Was Gabriel announcing a new life? To whom? To me?

I was sitting at the table surrounded by guests, flooded with feelings, intrigued and shaken, empowered and confused, amazed and deeply moved by this French-speaking, very pregnant woman who needed me and who had announced the imminent birth of a son.

I also felt like a tree whose roots had grown several yards deeper into the ground in the last few minutes, not a quantum leap, a quantum drop.

Oh, the unconscious activated! As if a gold mine had been tapped, ready to be exposed.

Nicole called me the next day. Over the next three weeks I drove to her home and gave her several bodywork treatments.

Nicole's passion had been classical ballet. She had trained extensively and had become a powerful dancer and performer with a strong musculature, not one of those anorexic tiny ballerinas. That was the problem. Nicole's body was very tight from taking on the sometimes abusive demands of ballet training. She told me what happened when she had tried to give birth to her first son. Her pelvic floor muscles could not relax and the birth canal could not dilate. After trying for hours and hours, she had had to give in and get a C-section. She was afraid the same scenario would happen again. She was very eager to experience natural childbirth. Could I help her?

The question was, could she undo years of tension in just a few sessions, so close to delivery time? Nicole did not want to attend prenatal groups. She insisted that she needed privacy, her own therapist, in her own space. I understood that she felt safe with me. I was French and for her represented the French classical ballet culture that had saved her life. It was agreed that I would coach her during labor.

Soon Nicole called me:

"*Peux-tu venir tout de suite?*" (Could you come right away?) It was early morning. I jumped in my car and rushed to Nicole's apartment. A midwife friend of Nicole's was with her; Jeremy and Zak had been sent out.

Nicole was having contractions. I spent the next five hours helping her stay with her breathing, use her voice to groan, moan, yell, scream, as my hands held her and pressed on her lower back. Was her pelvis going to relax, release, and open?

At the end of the day, she was only two centimeters dilated, too exhausted to continue. Feeling defeated, overcome with grief, distressed about the baby, she gave up. Jeremy drove her to Kaiser Oakland hospital, where she was told that she needed a C-section. The baby was large, more than eight pounds.

That evening, on May 3, 1987, Gaby was born.

Chapter 8

Neonatal Intensive Care Unit

Meditation

When I arrived at the hospital early the next morning, I expected to find Nicole and the baby together. There was a crib in Nicole's room but no baby. Nicole was still drugged and kept mumbling: "Where is my baby . . . Where is my baby? . . . I want my baby."

Panic-stricken, I managed to ask, "What happened?"

"She took him away . . . she took him away . . . " mumbled Nicole.

"Who took him away?" I asked.

"The nurse . . . the nurse . . . " She repeated, "Where is my baby?"

Nicole was not supposed to get up and walk yet, but she was about to do so when the nurse came into the room and explained, "Your baby needed oxygen. He is very sick. He was turning blue in his crib. His lungs needed immediate oxygen. He has to be monitored constantly; he is in the NICU." She added that she was not going to bring him back to Nicole's room.

Nicole screamed, "I need to see my baby, now, now, bring my baby back. I need to be with my baby. What are you doing to my baby? Bring my baby back."

The nurse finally gave in: better bring the baby for a moment! She came back holding a big bundle and placed it in Nicole's arms. This is how I saw Gaby for the first time. His eyes were closed, and he seemed in a deep trance; his face was very white. His mother calmed down as soon as she held him.

A moment of silence and timelessness filled the room. I breathed an immense sigh of relief.

Since she refused to get separated from her baby again, Nicole dragged herself out of bed, leaning on me, and followed the nurse back to the NICU. We entered the super-protected unit, clad in the required gowns.

In the NICU, Gaby was placed on his "bed," a little metal platform the size of a newborn, where he was kept naked, except for diapers, so that his little body could be seen by the nurse at all times. He was hooked to monitors with several tubes. There were eight other critically ill newborns in the big room, all on their little platforms, all hooked to monitors. Determined to stay with her baby, Nicole asked for a stool and sat next to him. I stood by the door, staring. Everything in the room was white, the walls, the floor, the nurses, the diapers on the babies, except for one tiny newborn who was black. I felt overwhelmed with sorrow and anguish, realizing I was staring at babies on the edge of life and death. That's when I got it, that sense of déjà vu, the white room, and the immobilized babies.

A female pediatrician arrived and started testing Gaby: spinal test, lung test, and brain test. Gaby had IVs in his head, his feet, his arms and wrists. He was drugged and was deep asleep during these pokings, prickings, and piercings of his little body. I kept staring, hiding the intense agitation welling up in me. Feeling that I was about to break down, I told Nicole I would be back tomorrow early morning. The nurse let me out.

I rushed home in time for my heart to burst open. I collapsed on my bed and sobbed. My body rolled in the fetal position and kept shaking. I had just seen essence and beauty. I was not seven anymore, and the newborn Gaby was not my baby brother, but I was terrified to lose him.

I got up very early the next morning to cook a big batch of brown rice for Nicole and arrived at the hospital by six A.M. Nicole had spent the whole night on the stool by Gaby's side. Her legs were swollen. She needed a break, but she was not going to move before I arrived, she told me. We agreed that one of us would always stay with Gaby in the NICU. We would not abandon him to the machines, monitors, and busy nurses.

I had brought food, fruit juices, and vitamins for the day. Nicole went back to her room to wash, eat, and sleep. And she needed to pump milk out of her breasts, which were beginning to hurt.

I took her place on the stool, ready to spend the rest of the day close to Gaby. This is when I connected with him. So far I had stayed focused on supporting Nicole. Now that she was resting, I was alone with Gaby for the first time and I could give him my full attention.

I kept looking at this exquisite-looking little being who showed no sign of pain; he was sedated. Gaby was a chubby baby, the image of a classic cherub, with tender peachy skin and soft tiny blond hair, a perfect round face and sweet features, fresh as dawn, a thing of beauty. I fell in love. But I was also dreadfully aware that his body was sick and hanging between life and death.

Very gently, I touched Gaby's tiny right hand, leaning slightly against his little platform bed, and kept still next to him. Then I took his hand in my big right hand, and kept holding it for a long time. I felt myself begin to relax, softening inside, layers of anxiety slowly washing away. I became more fully present, saying inwardly: I am here, you are here, we are together. I was feeling the tenderness of the moment spreading like melting butter inside me, touching and opening my heart space. I felt my body heat rising and my breathing getting deeper. I felt the sweet streams of energy I had experienced during deep meditations increasing within me, surging and spreading like electric currents through my whole body. I was getting filled with Shakti, gently bubbling through me and out of me. It was as if I was transferring into Gaby's little body my vigorous prana Shakti, or life force, accumulated over years of practice. I knew Gaby was receiving my energy, on some mysterious level that I could not see but I totally trusted.

Then I found myself whispering very soft sounds close to Gaby's ear. He had heard my voice before he was born and I knew that he would feel safe hearing it. Healing mantras my body had absorbed were oozing out of me, feeding our body and soul connection.

A fierce determination to keep Gaby alive arose in me. Could my concentration and my energies achieve this? I promised myself: "This one is not going to die."

Time stopped. I kept holding Gaby's hand until Nicole came back. She was ready to spend another night by Gaby's side. Jeremy, meanwhile, had to stay home and care for Zak.

I went home filled with my new love, my strong intention, and my full commitment.

Chapter 9

Divine Intervention

When I arrived early at the hospital on the third morning, the head pediatrician was standing outside the NICU and was ready to give Nicole the results of the tests. Gaby had a collapsed lung and was under heavy doses of antibiotic. His lung was not his only problem. Gaby had a blood mass in the middle of the left side of his brain from a stroke. He still had good reflexes, but the blood needed to be reabsorbed or else he would need brain surgery to remove it.

"Brain surgery, oh no," Nicole and I exclaimed, looking at each other horrified.

"Yes," the pediatrician added, "Gaby had three seizures on his first day at the NICU. His right foot and right hand were shaking. He was given anti-seizure medicine right away, that's why you never saw the seizures happen."

All of this was really hard to hear. I felt panic rising again, my whole body beginning to shake inside. I struggled to contain it, while Nicole was desperately trying to remain calm.

I left the hospital in a state of high alert and extreme urgency. What to do? Where to go? Where to find help? Who would understand? I got in my car, shaking, and found myself racing to the Oakland ashram, wishing my spiritual teacher were still alive. I could run to him and beg him for help, like many people had done for years. Miracles always happened around him, although he insisted he never performed them. But he had left his body five years ago.

His successor, a woman swami who embodied her teacher's spiritual power, happened to be staying at the Oakland ashram for a week. We had known one another at the Indian ashram and I had witnessed her transformation. I went to her, filled with intense anxiety, and I begged, "There is a newborn baby struggling for his life at the Oakland Kaiser hospital. His name is Gaby. He needs help. He needs all the blessings of the Siddhas."

She stared at me for a moment, and then she pronounced slowly these simple and powerful words: "You are the blessing!"

She turned to her assistant and made a sign. He handed her a small stuffed animal, which she handed to me, adding, "Take this to the baby."

It was a little tiger. I instantly understood. Gaby was my tiger cub and I was the tigress meant to fight for his survival and well-being. I felt that my prayer had been heard, and I left full of hope.

The fourth morning I was at the NICU very early. I was gowned again. The little stuffed tiger was wiped with disinfectant. I carried it to Gaby like the Holy Grail and placed it on his little platform bed against his right arm. He was four days old, asleep and adorable, but I knew that his right lung was struggling for oxygen and that his brain was in the process of a challenging recovery.

Nicole needed a break. I took my turn on the stool

and I spent several hours with Gaby holding his small hand, watching over him.

The message I had received was repeating itself in my mind like a mantra: "You are the blessing . . . you are the blessing . . . you are the blessing . . . ," sinking deeper and deeper inside my body and soul. These simple words were not just a hint, but a command from my spiritual teacher, the kind of mandate one does not question and puts into action here and now. It was telling me: "*You*, Odile, BE the blessing, *you* BE Gaby's blessing." I understood that this was the *seva* (selfless service) I had been given. My first task was to stay at Gaby's side, to stay one-pointed on Gaby's healing, to embody what I had been told, and keep trusting that my presence, physical and spiritual, was assisting him.

Although Gaby was asleep, I whispered words to his ear, repeating over and over again:

"May you receive the blessings this little tiger is bringing to you,

"May your brain be healed, may your lung be healed,

"May you be free of pain,

"May you be well and live a long healthy life."

I was not anxious anymore. I was not a powerless seven-year-old. I felt empowered. Gaby was cared for. He had his tiger and I had my commitment. Sitting next to Gaby became my meditation. I knew, right there and then, that our closeness was a blessing to both of us.

Later that day, Gaby was reexamined. His condition had improved. He was considered out of mortal danger and was moved to the intermediate unit. We were overjoyed.

He needed to be kept in an incubator until the antibiotic IV treatment was completed. He was too big for it. He kept fussing and crying, and had to be sedated again, but he was alive and he had even drunk a full bottle of his mother's pumped milk.

When the neurologist came by, he saw Gaby holding his tiger by the tail. Testing Gaby's reflex, he pulled on the tiger slightly and concluded: "Gaby has a good grip. That's a good sign. His stroke was mild. He looks good, considering what he has been through."

Gaby was four days old; he was a survivor. I was filled with thanks for all the help, for the medical help, for the spiritual help, for the flow of love, and for Gaby's own life force.

After spending the first fourteen days of his life at Kaiser Oakland, Gaby was finally ready to be released. Before he was discharged, the group of neonatologists who had followed him gave us their prognosis.

The good news was that Gaby's lung was fully healed. The bad news was that the blood clot in Gaby's left middle brain was still there, and the question was whether his body would absorb it or whether it would become a tumor, in which case surgery would be needed. They would not be able to tell before Gaby was six months old.

"Left brain damage," they explained, "might result in motor problems on the right side, speech problems, and reading difficulties. But a newborn brain, being so plastic, has the capacity to compensate for the damage and bounce back. Important functions lost can be transferred to other parts of the brain. But we cannot tell at this time what functions will be impaired. It could be fine motor movements, coordination of movements, gait. We cannot be sure until he grows up."

For us, the bad news was overshadowed by the fact that, here and now, Gaby was home and we could at last hold him. But deep down we worried about the brain clot and counted the weeks. After six months, the threat was over. No surgery was needed. Family, friends, caretakers, doctors—everybody had loved Gaby and whispered all kinds of sweet words to him. This spontaneous flow of tender loving care had surely been helping his wounded brain, and had eased the stress of the trauma.

Chapter 10

Becoming a Godmother

*"There is a natural joy when the heart opens to
its true nature."—Ajahn Sumedho*

W hen Gaby was finally home, I could not stop taking
photos of him. This was new to me. I had travelled
to remote exotic lands, but had never thought of taking a
camera with me; in fact, I had been dead against it.

In that picture-taking frenzy, I suddenly remembered
that the only photo I had ever seen of my baby brother was
the one on his memorial card. I knew I had saved one of
these cards, but where could it be? I eventually found it
in a trunk buried under all kinds of old mementos. As I
was staring at it, I saw the baby all in white, lying on his
crib with his little hands clasped on his chest and his eyes
closed, just the way I had seen him last, more than fifty
years ago. That's when I knew that I had to write our story.

Taking pictures of Gaby was my way of affirming over
and over again that here he was in front of me, flesh and
blood, for real. Gaby was photogenic. With his well-shaped
chubby baby body and his exquisite mother-of-pearl skin,
he was a perfect picture of the healthiest baby, his lovely
face so open it was hard to fathom that he had experienced
such deep trauma. His big eyes stared at me as if holding

on to mine, taking in every move I made. Gaby was fully present. I turned into his official archivist/photographer and Nicole nicknamed me "Kid Kodak."

That's also when I became Gaby's number-one babysitter and ordained myself as godmother, a beautiful title, which described exactly the one I wanted to become, a mother for the spirit, and Gaby became my godson, my child of spirit.

Nicole went back to work teaching ballet. Jeremy, a professional violinist, was busy trying to get as many gigs as he could to support his family, and Zak went to preschool. On her way to the dance studio, Nicole would bring Gaby to my home and pick him up a few hours later. I made a point to adjust my schedule to Nicole's. I was not going to miss any opportunity to care for our precious Gaby.

During that first year, holding Gaby, sometimes for a long time, became my meditation. I wrapped my arms around him and hugged him gently against my chest. This way he could feel my heartbeat the way he had felt his mother's in the womb, and I could listen to his heartbeat against my own heart. When I felt our hearts beating in unison, I was overjoyed, in a state of pure loving and timeless oneness.

I would also rock him gently and talk to him, not baby talk, but stories and songs, in French or English, and mantras in Sanskrit. He stared at me as if fascinated and comforted by my voice. During these first warm summer months, I made a point of wearing tank tops and of keeping Gaby naked except for diapers so that we could have skin-to-skin contact.

I also kept in mind that Gaby's stroke had affected his left brain. I would place my hands on his skull, and maintain this gentle contact, as if communicating with his brain, and encouraging it to keep finding new neural pathways. It was a delight to watch Gaby's face become more and more beautiful as I became more and more present. I would also bring my hands to his right leg and foot, or his right arm and hand, making deep loving contact to stimulate all the inner connections between brain and limbs. I could see that Gaby loved this kind of total attention.

When Gaby fell asleep in my arms, rather than putting him back to bed, I kept holding him in my lap. This took me into a deep meditative state. I was in awe of how blissful I felt. What was it that made me feel so good? I asked myself. Was it the tenderness of Gaby's skin in my hands? The deep relaxation and peace of mind that took over my whole being? The fact that I was so totally absorbed in the moment? The release of oxytocin? Was it noticing that our breathing had become one breath?

Here I was, forty-four years later, holding an infant again, just as I had done as a child, filled with love, sometimes with tears running down my cheeks, thrilled to have him for hours while everyone was out and busy. The spontaneous awakening of love I had experienced in meditation for no one in particular was now finding someone who needed a lot of care and plenty of loving presence, to feel safe and to keep growing.

I was now practicing the Rosen Method Bodywork modality. I was transforming my hands into antennas, listening to another's emotional body deep inside their physical body, and transmitting loving support to help them sink into their self-experience. My awareness kept increasing as I held Gaby and noticed how he thrived receiving this conscious contact. We were growing together. I was helping Gaby feel himself, and Gaby was helping me become more attuned to another being. We were supporting one another.

I also understood I was redoing my own childhood, giving to Gaby what I had not received, the care and contact that was missing in the way I was raised, the so-called detached way. As a newborn, I already had my own bedroom, next to the room of my first nanny, whom I had called Bille. My parents would see me once a day when Bille would bring me to the living room for them to kiss the baby goodnight. No breastfeeding, no cuddling, no holding or sitting on laps, no hugging from my mother, who was not interested and had handed me to Bille. Bille was with me until the declaration of war, but because she was a German-Swiss citizen, it was not safe for her to stay in France. One morning I was told that she had left for good. Abandoned at four by the only caring person I knew, and passed on to a stranger, the next nanny, I became an island unto myself, except for the very brief time when I had fallen in love with my baby brother.

My mother had also been raised by nannies, servants, and nuns, just like me and my siblings. Her father had died before she was born, and her young widowed mother never recovered, falling into such deep mourning that she could not take care of her three needy kids. My mother gave birth to seven children. After the death of her first son, she had one more girl, and then finally ten years later she had another son. But, for her, children were a chore that she managed to avoid because she could afford to hire nannies and, as soon as we were old enough, send us to boarding school. Like her mother, she had no caring in her to give.

Later, when Gaby was walking, he invented a new a game we both loved.

My living room then was a long narrow room with windows at both ends, one facing sunrise and the other facing sunset. I kept the center of the room empty and spacious for my practice of movement, dancing, and yoga.

That's where Gaby discovered the fun of running. The wall-to-wall carpeted floor was safe, and the length of the room gave him plenty of space to practice. I squatted on the floor at one end of the room with my arms wide open. From the other end of the room Gaby would run towards me, cautiously at first. I would catch him, hold him for a moment, and then he would run right back to the other end of the room and start all over again, each time running a little faster. At some point Gaby was running so fast, he would throw himself into my arms, laughing ecstatically. He could spend the whole afternoon repeating this same game, pushing his limits, getting more and more excited, discovering himself: "Look how fast I can run! See, how my right foot works! My legs are good and strong! Very cool!"

This game went on for weeks. Every time he came to my home, he would say, with his usual determination, "Running game!"

Of course I was thrilled! It was fun and it was just what I needed. Reopening the heart, I had learned, after it had been traumatized, was a life-long process. Marion Rosen, the founder of the Rosen Method and author of the book *Rosen Method Bodywork: Accessing the Unconscious Through Touch*, explained that "the longest lasting barriers [chronic muscle tensions] often result from the loss of a parent through death, when one is still a child . . . The family is so taken up with the activity surrounding the event that the child is not listened to and her feelings are overlooked." In my case, it was the loss of my baby brother, and not only my feelings but also my very existence in the family, that had been overlooked.

There was still a deep clutching inside my chest. Slowly I was allowing this barrier to soften when receiving private Rosen Method Bodywork treatments.

"Yes," I responded to my practitioner during a session, "my seven-year-old arms and chest which had held the baby were suddenly empty, and I clutched my arms against my chest in my bed at night to avoid feeling the emptiness and the loneliness, in my lonely bedroom, with no one to love anymore."

This awareness of my body was helpful, but the greatest help came from feeling Gaby's chubby body rushing into my open arms and pounding against my heart, over and over again. It made my ribcage shake and explode, my voice burst out with huge sounds, my whole chest shriek and roar with laughter. Gaby found my reactions very funny. It was as if he was mysteriously guided by some universal healing force—Shakti power—to knock at my wall and break it open for good. Yes, Gaby was my healer. We were healing one another.

Godmother-godson

Chapter 11

My Doctor Rosen, Forty Years Later

*"Synchronicity is an ever present reality for those
who have eyes to see."*—Carl Jung

The years 1986 and 1987 were defining years. The death of my mother, the birth of Gaby, and my choice of the Rosen Method as my new life's calling all came together.

After I reconnected with my mother, thanks to the physical contact she needed from me, my path had become obvious. I wanted to understand the healing power of touch and continue to communicate with people through touch.

As soon as I returned from my mother's funeral, I decided to take up the Rosen Method Bodywork training. I had heard of the Rosen Method as soon as I settled in Berkeley. One of my new friends was going through the training at that time and had offered to give me free sessions as part of her practicum. She introduced me to Marion Rosen, who also had given me a few private sessions. I had felt, deep inside, the power of gentle touch to reach the unconscious emotional wounds repressed in my body and heal them.

My previous studies in psychology and yoga were a good preparation for a body/mind/heart/spirit therapy. Equally useful was my longtime meditation practice.

However, I needed some official certification to become a legitimate professional in this country. My diplomas and credentials in psychology, psychotherapy, and yoga therapy had been awarded in France and in India.

I also recognized that my Rosen Method practice had really started spontaneously when I was holding my mother and sitting at her bedside before her death. A year later, sitting with Gaby, at his side in the NICU room, I experienced how loving hands could support his body's self-healing. My mother and Gaby had been my first patients and had invited me to reinvent myself as a healing touch therapist.

After three years of training, I began to see my first clients. One of my friends referred Bernie to me, a gentle and lovely man in his forties who worked as a member of the coast guard and wrote poetry. He needed to learn how to relax painful chronic tensions, letting go of deep unresolved emotional pain stored in his body. He came to me every week. My hands would contact his chest and soon he would weep, releasing all the crying he had had to stuff away as a boy. He was amazed at his reactions, while I was again in awe at the profound impact of conscious touch.

One evening after giving Bernie his weekly session, I went out for a walk in my lovely neighborhood. I was musing, "This work is really something I can do . . . I feel wonderful and open after giving sessions . . . I love doing it . . . My clients appreciate this . . . and I can earn my living doing it . . . I am so fortunate!"

As I enjoyed my stroll, inhaling the jasmine-scented air on Russell Street, I was startled by a vision-like memory.

Who appeared to me but Dr. Rosen, *mon Docteur Rosen,* my loving Dr. Rosen who had spent so much time with me when I was ill as a child.

The vision welling up from my forgotten past was becoming clear. I saw Dr. Rosen's black eyes looking back at me as he left my lonely room, smiling tenderly at me and telling me that he would come back tomorrow. I could see myself in bed, desperately holding on to his words, not wanting him to go, pleading inside, "Yes, please come back."

Dr. Rosen, Rosen Method, the same name! What a surprise! Why had I not made the connection earlier?

In a flash, I understood it all. I saw myself sitting next to the massage table with my hands on Bernie's chest, just like Dr. Rosen had sat next to me. Bernie kept his eyes closed, but at times he turned his head toward me and looked at me. I could see he was deeply moved, and as I looked back at him, a wave of tenderness brought tears to my eyes. We were sharing the same field of love. Dr. Rosen all over again! I had unknowingly embodied my childhood Dr. Rosen.

I understood why I had embraced the Rosen Method training with such confidence. Although I had heard the word "Rosen" hundreds of times in the last three years, I had not recognized the link. The word "Rosen" sounded so different when pronounced with a French accent. But the name Rosen had subconsciously drawn me in. It had triggered a compelling response deep inside me. The kind of touch, gentle and non-manipulative, the listening with my hands to the breath, encouraging the emotions held in the body to be felt, responding with compassionate words, all kept telling me that I had found what I had been searching for a long time.

Perhaps because I had missed Dr. Rosen so much, my innocent psyche had decided to become like him. Maybe that had been my way to keep the spiritual presence of Dr. Rosen in my life.

Now I had taken his seat. I could give to others the healing touch I had received from him. I remembered he had told me that souls continue to communicate after death, so I could tell him: "Not only did you heal my lung and my loneliness. You gave me a role model to hold on to. You were my first mentor. Your example led me to this powerful form of healing, which by some strange coincidence, wears your name."

Chapter 12

I Am Your Brother

Gaby's family, Mom, Dad, and brother Zak, moved from Oakland to an apartment on Delaware Street in North Berkeley. At exactly the same time, a good friend, leaving her North Berkeley cottage on Spruce Street, arranged to pass it on to me. Gaby, then four years old, and I became neighbors without having had to plan it.

This little house felt like my first real home. It met my need for a simple life, surrounded by nature, and became a sacred haven for me, a healing temple for my patients, and a playground for Gaby. Tucked away between three other cottages, and surrounded by a tall cedar tree, a huge oak tree, and plenty of lavender, jasmine, and laurel bushes, it was quiet and charming.

Then Gaby started going to preschool at the Jewish Community Center (JCC) on Walnut Street, a five-minute walk from my new home. I always noticed and loved these kinds of signs and wondered about them. Providence or Shakti was bringing us together, closer and closer.

I often picked Gaby up at the JCC around three P.M., and we would drive off to Tilden Park.

Tilden Park, at the top of the Berkeley Hills, had become my country home. I explored its canyons and creeks, its fire trails and hiking trails. I had my favorite trees and groves, and even a secret garden. I had special walks for every time of the day or night, for rainy days and sunny days. Some were solitary walks, and some were walks shared by others. Once Gaby saw the ducks on Jewel Lake and discovered the Little Farm, he also became a fan.

One day, when Gaby had settled in the car, I asked, "Gaby, where do you want to go today?"

"To the Little Farm," was his instant answer. His language was still very simple, his sentences short.

On the way, we stopped at my house to get some celery for the cows, an important part of the ritual. Then we drove up the gentle slope of Spruce Street, the beautiful three miles running parallel to our magnificent Bay. Spring was gorgeous in our neighborhood, the streets fragrant with magnolias and jasmines, and the road to Tilden Park an urban pleasure.

I was driving slowly, feeling happy to spend a few hours with playful Gaby. He was a big boy, tall and strong, and could use the seatbelt instead of the child seat. So we were both sitting in front. Suddenly, without any preliminary, I heard Gaby declare loud and clear, "I am your brother." He said it matter-of-factly, a piece of information he was passing on.

I was startled. I took a deep breath, kept holding on to the steering wheel and staring at the road. Then I looked at Gaby. He kept staring at the road too and did not seem to expect a response. He had delivered his message, and he was done. It wasn't something he figured out, or remembered; it just came to him and was put into words before he knew it.

I went along, curious about where this would take us, and confirmed, "Well, yes Gaby, you are my brother."

And that was settled. We arrived at the Little Farm. Gaby ran to his two favorite cows, then ran to Jewel Lake, where he called on the ducks, then ran back to the car, all according to our afternoon ritual.

Later, after taking Gaby home, still mesmerized by his announcement, I called my spiritual friend Lynn, both of us disciples of the same spiritual teacher and versed in the same Eastern philosophies. When I told her what Gaby had declared, her tone of voice became very serious.

"We have to believe these things," she asserted. "They are signs we are given."

"Signs of what?" I asked.

"Signs of recognition," she suggested. "But tell me," she inquired, "what was it like for you to hear this?"

"I still feel shaken," I answered. "I feel my heart pounding, my chest is vibrating deep inside as if touched by an angel, I am at a loss for words, and at the same time I feel exhilarated, almost changed."

"Of course," said Lynn, who knew my family history. "I would too, but try to tell me more. How does it make you feel about Gaby?"

"Well, I have been devoted to Gaby ever since he was born, as you know, and it's been wonderful, but I was a little hesitant and cautious not to intrude in the family dynamic. I think I was holding back. Now he is telling me that he and I have our own connection in some mysterious way. I might feel more at ease, more free."

"Sure," said Lynn, "that's it. Feel free. Don't hold back."

"Also," I added, "it makes me want to explore the signs, as you call them."

So I did some research and found out that there are plenty of children who remember past lives and tell their parents. Children generally talk about their past when they are between ages of two and seven, sometimes as soon as they can talk. Later they forget about it as they get more involved in present time and their ego gets stronger.

This seemed to be what had happened with Gaby, who was four. He could talk well enough to put this information into words. In fact, he talked about it several times again the same year. He would say, "You are my godmother, and I am your brother." Each time I felt touched all over again.

Gaby always mentioned it in the car, sitting next to me. That made sense. We tend to go into a light trance when we are a passenger. In that state the conscious mind is dimmed; subconscious knowing surfaces easily, especially in young children, and spontaneous statements can come through.

What's more, sitting in the car was about the only time Gaby kept still. As soon as he was out, he was busy running, playing ball, and inventing games.

Wanting to test how strong this connection was for him, I said to him one day, "Gaby, we are good friends. I am your friend and you are my friend, it makes me very happy."

He instantly corrected me. "I am your brother," he said, with a tinge of pride in his voice, as if to tell me he knew better.

And what of reincarnation, I asked myself? My first

thought was of my baby brother who had died in my arms in 1944, forty-six years earlier! From my studies of Hinduism and Buddhism, I had adopted the concept of reincarnation, but I had never had direct experiences, although the first time I landed in India I had such a strong sense of déjà vu that I assumed I had spent past lives there and was coming back home.

Wishing for more feedback, I even got a reading, unusual for me, from a psychic I will call D, who had been well-known in the seventies as one of Michael's channels. Michael was an ancient entity who spoke through gifted channels. This is what D said, which I recorded: "These two fragments (you and Gaby) are entity mates and share some fifteen past associations, not the least of which was as fellow artists who were struggling, but who supported each other through a mutual pact regarding income. In that instance, Odile, this little fragment (Gaby) contributed more to your well-being than you did to his. It was he who made the money, and he supported you in many ways, but joyfully; there was no sacrifice and negativity on his part. What you are experiencing now is a remembrance of those good times and an opportunity to do something for him. And one more thing: this was in France, so you at least had one lifetime together in France. It sounds wonderful," D added in a more personal tone. "Enjoy him."

I listened to the recording over and over again, allowing myself to trust more and more the depth of my bond with Gaby. But the most important words that I kept hearing were "Enjoy him," echoing in my whole being, just like the earlier message I had received when Gaby was a new-born: "You are the blessing." This was my new and next assignment: "Enjoy him."

Joy had been so lacking in my growing-up that I had forgotten it could be part of my own experience. Of course I had known moments of pleasure and fun before as an adult, but it mostly felt like a feeling of relief that would not last. The kind of joy that is pure, easy, spontaneous, I had not really allowed myself to feel and trust.

"Gaby is the source of joy," I had to tell myself, "take it in; it's not just Gaby's joy, it's also yours to have, to feel, to grow, to spread." Learning to be more aware of joy, and to stay with joyful moments, became another meditation practice. Gaby was teaching me joy!

Chapter 13

Gaby's Healers, Role Models

"The wound is the place where the Light enters you."—Rumi

Nicole and I had noticed that Gaby, still a baby in his crib, favored his left hand. He was always reaching out for his toys or his feet with his left hand, while his right hand remained uninvolved. And when he started crawling, it was obvious that his left leg was doing the crawling while his right one was not doing much.

Gaby entered a cycle of biweekly sessions with a wonderful young occupational therapist, Diane, at the Fruitvale Health Center.

I used to take Gaby to these sessions. Rather than drop him off and pick him up an hour later, I sat on the floor, in a corner of the big playroom, watching and listening.

In her late twenties, Diane was a dark-eyed Irish pixie who exuded vitality. She took Gaby through a series of exercises to enlist his right side.

What was fascinating to me was how she related to Gaby. She made sure to look at him and connect with him, with love and joy in her eyes. She made sure every exercise was playful. She was here to play with him; they were playmates, playing together. She seemed to have nothing better to do than play with Gaby. I loved watching them.

For example, in order to teach Gaby to use his right hand, arm, and shoulder, Diane would get him to lie on his stomach on top of a big ball, and then she kept the ball rolling back and forth. From this perch on the ball, Gaby had to reach out and pick up a toy on the floor with his right hand. He did it over and over again, laughing as if he were on a roller coaster.

As he kept rolling faster and would be about to fall off the ball, he would have to catch himself with his right hand. Diane kept calling out, "Gaby, what is your right hand doing? . . . Is your right hand having fun too?" . . . over and over, making a song out of it, as if she was serenading him. She never rushed him. She always marveled at him. Diane also had to teach Gaby to use his right leg. He loved crawling and could crawl fast enough to have fun, but his right leg would drag behind.

Diane would get him on all fours. She would stand behind him, hold his pelvis with both hands, and get his right knee to lead the way. She turned the exercise into a chasing game, Gaby trying to crawl away from Diane's hold and Diane holding on to him.

Watching them, I was learning about special needs and recovery, but what touched me the most was the beauty of the therapeutic relationship as demonstrated by Diane: her creativity, her enthusiasm, and her playfulness. She knew how to enjoy him and how to enjoy herself.

Diane was not intent on fixing Gaby, she was here to play with him. When the game worked out, she was as excited as he was. If it did not work out, she was never disappointed.

Diane was already a healer. She became a new role model for me. I had never witnessed anyone like her, so thrilled to spend time with a patient. At that time, I was beginning my private practice as a bodywork therapist, seeing clients and taking my work very seriously. Diane inspired me to express not only my skills and competence, but also my love of the work, and the joy I felt when connecting with my clients.

I also noticed that during the sessions Gaby would turn to me, look at me, and meet my eyes. He was making sure I was watching him. I would beam silently. He could see that I was delighted watching him discover all kinds of new small skills. It was clear that my presence, even quiet, affirmed and amplified his experience of himself.

When Gaby started standing up, it became obvious how spastic the whole right side of his body was. His right arm would shoot straight up involuntarily, like a kid raising his hand in class. He could bring it down, but for several years he had to be constantly reminded.

"Gaby, what is your right arm doing?" we asked playfully.

Also his right hand stayed stuck in a fist, with the thumb inside the hand.

"Gaby, where is your thumb?" we asked.

He would look at his fist as if he was reconnecting with a stranger, open his hand, see his thumb and exclaim with glee, "There it is."

Nicole and I made a point of keeping it playful, never saying "Drop your arm" or "Open your fist," learning to ask him a fun question rather than telling him what to do. This was new and healing for me, coming from an educational background where kids were ordered around every step of the way.

At this time, Gaby's family lived on a second-floor apartment, and the stairs were carpeted but steep. At first Gaby would go down on his butt like most little kids do, but soon he wanted to do it standing up like his brother.

Diane taught him how to go down safely, holding the railing with both hands. When we tried to help, Gaby would get very upset and say forcefully, "By myself!" This was his new mantra: "By myself!" Gaby loved to figure out how to do new things, taking his time, and we made sure to never rush him.

This "by myself" resonated with a part of me, the one who had been determined from age seven to find her own way and keep pushing against rules and conventions.

The first time Gaby, a child who had a stroke as a newborn, took his first steps by himself without holding on to anything is something I will remember forever.

It was at his grandmother Ellie's home, in the Oakland hills, on a sunny summer afternoon. I was standing on the deck. Gaby was standing at the threshold between the living room and the deck, holding on to the frame of the sliding door with both hands.

"Gaby, I want to take a picture of you on the deck," I said, holding the camera with one hand and extending my other hand toward him. "Could you step forward a little bit?"

I saw Gaby focus, let go one hand at a time. Then, keeping his arms up shoulder-height like a tightrope acrobat, he fixed his gaze on my extended hand, walked cautiously toward me and took my hand.

With tears in my eyes, I clicked quietly to record this special moment. I remember him fully absorbed, holding on to the energetic thread connecting us and trusting it would take him across the three feet to reach me. Once he was on the deck, he let go of my hand and kept taking a few steps toward one chair, then another chair a little further away, and kept going, at his own slow careful pace, totally absorbed in his new experience. I kept watching him and finally he turned to me. "Yes Gaby, by yourself !" I confirmed with conviction.

Yes, Gaby was walking, but with a limp. He could not put his right foot flat on the ground; he was walking on its outer edge and dragging it. It was time to take him to the local Shriners Hospital.

The Shriners Hospital for Children is a remarkable institution, the official philanthropy of the Shriners, a fraternal organization, based on brotherly love and the enjoyment of life through service.

The hospitals were first formed to treat young victims of polio, and later came to deal with all pediatric cases, most especially with orthopedic injuries and acute burns. There was never any charge, and they pioneered the newest treatments.

In order to be admitted as a patient, a child had to be sponsored by a Shriner. Nicole found out that there was a Shriner who owned a barbershop two blocks from their home. He was happy to sponsor Gaby and signed the forms.

Walking into the big hospital lobby, full of light and colorful decorations, was a shock of contrasts. I saw children come in with horrendous problems, and at the same time I noticed the big smiles on all the faces of the staff welcoming them.

I immediately got the message: first acknowledge the child, whatever state she/he is in, see the divine child in him/her, welcome them with love, see the pathology later.

The first visit lasted three hours, and Gaby continued to be treated there every week, later every month, until he was eighteen years old.

I went to many appointments with him, and again I watched and listened.

The Shriners staff, like Diane, created an immediate rapport with Gaby. They welcomed him each time as if they were greeting a favorite family member. Even at his very young age, they addressed him first and directly, almost ignoring us adults accompanying him.

They always told Gaby ahead of time what their medical plan was, explaining to him in detail what the procedure would be and what its purpose was. They warned him whether it would hurt and for how long. They asked for his permission to go ahead, checking with him if he had any questions. When Gaby did, they listened religiously. And they always validated him, rewarded him, and loved him.

All the staff exemplified the Shriners' dedication to serving people in need. This became another of my mantras and assignments: the enjoyment of life through service.

To actually feel the power of love running the hospital and to see the *joie de vivre* of the staff was a new experience for me. Except for a short-lived glimpse of love from Dr. Rosen when I was a child, I had never seen such joy on the faces of my educators, doctors, or helpers, who were considered the most competent in their fields, but never expressed enjoyment at seeing me.

During Gaby's first visit, Dr. Skinner, an older, white, easygoing orthopedic surgeon, and his team of three specialists spent a lot of time observing how Gaby walked, asking him to try different steps, forward, backward, sideways, up and down the long hallway, in order to analyze the distortions in his gait.

Dr. Skinner explained to Gaby, with Nicole and me present in the room, that he was walking on his anklebone because there was no muscle holding his ankle. Since his bones were growing, his anklebone would soon get deformed. The treatment would consist of a specific surgery, a tibial tendon transfer. But before the surgery, the tendons and the muscles needed to be stretched to allow the foot to stay in the correct position after the surgery.

When we heard the word "stretch," Nicole and I, in the background, looked at one another anxiously, just the kind of parental reaction a child should not have to deal with, and I understood why we were always removed from the doctor/patient rapport.

Next Gaby was off to the cast room, where George greeted him as if he was his best friend. George was the stretching and casting therapist. He had to stretch Gaby's foot muscles, and while he was pulling them, his assistant would wrap a cast around the ankle to maintain the stretch in place. This had to be repeated every month for the next five years. These elongations, although done gradually, were very painful for Gaby. But George, a large, handsome African American man with big, powerful hands, was so cheerful it was contagious. First he would take Gaby through a clowning routine. They laughed together. George kept entertaining and distracting Gaby while performing the horrendous stretches. After the session, Gaby remembered George's jokes rather than his pain, and even looked forward to his next visit. That was George's secret, jollity, a funny new word and a new attitude for me to take in. I could see that once Gaby was relaxed and giggling with George, he paid less attention to the pain.

Gaby, now four, went to his first pre-K class with his cast on, but covered by a boot and long pants. He did not want the kids to see it. He did not want to look different.

One day, Nicole and I were driving back from the hospital. Gaby had his new cast on. Every month, he could choose a different color cast. For this one he had chosen a black one because it was Halloween! Suddenly Gaby started sobbing.

"What's wrong, Gaby?" we asked.

"Everyone is going to know who I am," he said, very upset.

Of course, all the fun of getting a fancy Halloween costume was to be unrecognizable. He dreaded that his cast would give him away on his trick-or-treat night.

"Oh Gaby, don't worry, we'll figure out a special outfit for you."

That's how Gaby became a caveman, covered with rags and more rags wrapped around his legs and feet, hiding all signs of his cast.

At age eight, Gaby was ready for the next procedures. The surgeon and his team needed to figure out which of his ankle muscles were working and which were not working, before they could decide on the appropriate surgery.

They placed electrodes on Gaby's right leg, and then asked him to walk. While Gaby was walking, they sent electric currents to the different muscles in his leg in order to read on a computer monitor which muscles had fired and which had not.

They also had to find out which muscles were the strongest. With Gaby sitting, they sent stronger and stronger electric currents into his leg muscles to check how much charge each reacted to. Again, this was very painful for Gaby, but they kept acknowledging his courage and his willingness, and made Gaby feel proud of himself rather than distressed by the pain.

I watched quietly in the background, feeling anxious but learning to remain as positive and enthusiastic as the doctors, internalizing "enjoying life through service" and trusting that my presence was part of the service. I kept hearing the message given to me when Gaby was a newborn, "You are the blessing," and knew my task was to discover at every step how to be the blessing Gaby needed at that moment.

Finally, in September 1995, Gaby's leg was ready for surgery. It consisted of splitting the tendon into two halves. One half would stay in place and the other half would be attached to the weaker muscle. The surgeon had to make five incisions around Gaby's ankle.

I saw Gaby in the recovery room the next day. He was on his hospital bed, wearing a pink T-shirt, green shorts, and a huge turquoise-colored cast from toes to knee. He looked like a prince, with balloons floating around his bed and his legs raised on silky pillows, handsome, proud, radiant, surrounded by his court. He was on morphine and was thrilled with the attention and the gifts. It was a party.

I brought Gaby a present that I had crafted especially for the occasion. It was a collage made of many cut-out magazine photos of cheetahs, cheetahs running, cheetahs grooming one another, a cheetah mum with her three cubs, a cheetah on a full moon night, combined with sliced photos of Gaby, all collaged together.

I knew cheetahs played an important role in Gaby's psyche. For his sixth birthday, I had asked him, "Gaby, what would you like for your birthday?"

"I want a cheetah," he had shot back with such energy that it sent me on a mission running all over town to various kids' stores to find one. At the last minute I bought one at the Sierra Club store, a beautiful stuffed animal that Gaby called Chitti and adopted as his alter ego.

I had subscribed to *Zoobooks*, a gorgeous monthly magazine for children, each issue focused on one animal species. Cheetahs had become Gaby's favorite, and we would read about them over and over again. Gaby stared at the picture of a cheetah running at top speed and said, "Look, Didi, he is flying!" He was riveted.

Gaby had learned that cheetahs were the fastest animals on land. We also read that they were very different from other big cats: they did not roar and did not fight. Cheetahs were so gentle that some people kept them as pets. Moreover, cheetah mothers were very protective of their young, and cheetah families were very close. And on top of all that, cheetahs needed our protection. It was clear that Gaby identified with cheetahs. When he told me, "They are very special!" it was as if he was telling me, "I am very special," and, of course, I fully responded: "Yes, they are very, very special."

I assembled the collage while Gaby was going through the surgery. It was my way of staying energetically focused on Gaby's well-being, sending him love and praying for a good outcome. I framed it and wrote on the back, "For Gaby, your power animal brings you love and energy for a prompt recovery."

Staring at it, reading the dedication, Gaby was mesmerized, and finally exploded "Cheetahs!" at the top of his drugged lungs. That said it all.

And then, from his bed, with his big cast on, he added, "I am going to show you how fast I can go!"

He got us to carry him to a powered wheelchair, the kind with an extension so his right leg could be supported. He settled in, and off he went down the long hall, yelling, "See how fast I can go!" He had no leg power at the moment, but he had arms and wheels, and speed was still possible. Here he was, a cheetah on wheels!

The next day, Nicole told me a funny Gaby story. She had stayed with him, and in the middle of the night, Gaby woke up his mother.

"Gaby, what's wrong? Are you in pain?"

Shaking and sobbing, he managed to explain, "They made a mistake. They put my heart in my ankle."

Nicole understood. "Oh, Gaby, it feels like your heart, but it's not your heart. I know what you mean, it's throbbing all around your ankle, it feels like it's your heart beating, but it's OK. It's normal; it's the blood rushing to your ankle to help it recover. It's a good sign."

"Oh!" said Gaby, and went right back to sleep.

On the second day, Alvin, the physical therapist, had to stand Gaby up on both feet and get him to walk, to avoid blood clots. It was going to be excruciating, but again, because Alvin was able to make it a special adventure, Gaby went through it, focusing on Alvin's strength, support, and love rather than on the pain.

After four days at the hospital, and off the morphine, Gaby was back home and found a surprise.

Since he still had to sit in bed most of the day with his leg elevated, I found an electric hospital bed for him. The family that had it put away in their garage was happy to get rid of it, as long as we could figure out a way of transporting this monstrously clunky load. I got help from my friends, two strong and very kind guys who worked in construction and had a big van. Being Gaby's blessing in any small way was my joy.

The bed was a great toy. Gaby would hold the electric button and play at raising the bed in different positions, thrilled that he had some power, power over the bed's motor. And he loved to show it off to friends who came to visit.

Soon, Gaby was learning to walk around the house with his big cast on and with the help of a walker. He was eager to go back to school but he was not going to be seen walking with a prop.

"I am not taking my walker to school," he announced.

"You are going to walk by yourself?" Nicole asked, surprised and concerned.

"Yep," affirmed Gaby. He wore long thick sweat pants, thick socks and big sneakers, to hide the cast, and off he went, limping and confident.

When the big cast came off his right leg, Gaby could put the sole of his foot flat on the ground, but all in one piece. He still could not do the normal heel-then-toes roll like the other foot. It was not perfect, but it was a huge improvement. He walked with a slight limp and that's how he is still walking today.

He kept going to the Shriners, where his beloved helpers greeted him like a star. He still needed to wear a day brace for several months, and then a night brace. But eventually at age eighteen, when he became too old to be their patient, he had to say goodbye to the Shriners.

For me, watching the Shriners in action had been a major paradigm shift, and well timed, as I was becoming a healing agent myself.

Gaby had internalized the Shriners' general attitude of optimism, jollity, love, and service. He had been fully validated, admired, and loved by his healers and had become a proud and happy young man. But there were still times when he felt pain in his right foot. He was growing, and his six-foot-tall body was getting heavier on his feet. How was he going to get through the rest of his life with a painful ankle? Who was going to help?

We met Gail. Gail, a physical therapist who loved kids with special needs, was another cheerful mentor for both Gaby and me. She welcomed Gaby with a big smile and an open heart, and he fell for her instantly. He went for his first visit with a lot of pain, and came out ready to shoot baskets in his backyard hoop. He was not pain-free but could override it. How could this happen?

To understand, I kept taking Gaby, now nineteen, to Gail's office, where I watched and listened. Gaby had experienced his body through pain. Feeling pain, avoiding pain, enduring pain, managing pain. Now, instead of stretching a foot, exercising an arm or a leg, or loosening a fist, Gail would rock Gaby's back very slowly on a low massage table, ask him to feel his torso in contact with the table, guiding him to sense his whole body, and the connections between all the parts of his body. Based on the Feldenkrais Method of somatic education, she taught Gaby to feel himself, to sense his body through slow, steady, gentle, deliberate movement

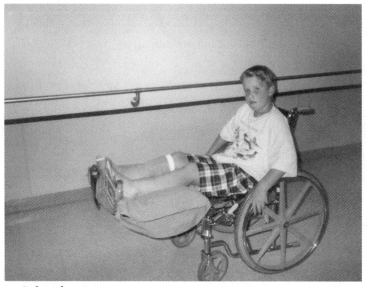

Gaby after surgery

as she enlisted his awareness. Gaby found out that walking was about his whole body, not just his foot, and gradually he noticed he could walk with less and less pain.

That changed the quality of his life altogether, and it showed me again and again how important it was to keep in mind the whole person when connecting with one part of the body. Again I was in awe at the therapeutic relationship. Gaby loved receiving this new kind of attention, given by a focused, nurturing, loving healer who enjoyed herself doing it.

For many more months Gaby wore a newly invented type of leg brace, not a cast but a soft, flexible boot in which the ankle could bend. Finally he quit trying to improve his ankle. He said he was getting used to the pain. Maybe it was his way of saying that he was not focused on the pain anymore. He had integrated all the changes set in motion during the treatments. He had developed a new awareness of himself and of his options. For years he had received such positive messages about who he was that his limp became less and less important to him.

Actually, it became his own original distinctive feature.

Chapter 14

Listening to Lake Temescal

"Play is our brain's favorite way of learning."
—Diane Ackerman

I discovered Oakland's Lake Temescal all by myself the third year I was living in the East Bay. One fresh and clear morning, I was driving down Broadway Terrace, a mile-long winding road. At the bottom of the hill, a clump of redwood trees drew my attention; I made a sharp U-turn and found myself at some mysterious gate; here was a dark path going under a dark tunnel, and on the other side of the tunnel, a lovely grove of redwoods and a few parking spots with only three other cars, and no one around. I was intrigued!

I stepped gently into this newfound land, walking like a cat, so I would not disturb the silence. I felt I had happened on a magic spot. It was quiet as a church. My eyes, wide open, suddenly saw the lake appear under the branches of two weeping willows. Like a magnet, the lake drew me in and I fell in love with Lake Temescal.

I walked around the lake according to the traditional Hindu ritual called *pradakshina*, keeping the lake to my right side as my object of worship, and circumambulating it at least one time on each visit and sometimes twice or any number of times.

I was also curious about the name Temescal, a strong word. I found out it was an Aztec word meaning "sweat house," given to the Temescal creek by the Costanoan Indians. The lake was like a gem nestled between hills, surrounded and protected by trees, like a nature womb, feeling intimate and luscious.

I never shared my special relationship with Lake Temescal until I went there with Gaby. He was about five years old by then. Gaby had a day off from kindergarten. It was a sunny winter morning.

I wanted Gaby to discover the lake the way I had, by the back door, where the ancient trees had invited me in. As soon as Gaby saw the lake, he ran freely toward it, across the thick green meadow. At the edge of the lake, he stopped and stared. We stared together. The water was a soft blue, reflecting the winter sky, or soft green, reflecting trees and shrubs. The light breeze played softly with the surface of the lake. That was the moment of awe and wonder I had experienced here and had wished for Gaby. We stared until a duck came gliding by.

Gaby waved to the duck, trying to get its attention, calling to it: "Come here!" It did not work; the duck kept ignoring us.

"Didi, let's pick some rocks," Gaby decided.

"OK, but let's find small rocks," I replied. "Let's walk around the lake and look for a good spot."

We got to a little patch of sand at the edge of the water between a bunch of high reeds, under the shade of an old, thick willow tree. We sat down side by side, with our hands full of tiny rocks, and we discovered a new game.

Gaby would throw a rock. We listened to the sound it made as it hit the water, and we tried to repeat the sound with our voices. We got into the old call-and-response chanting form, the call coming from the splash and the response from our voices.

At first it was kind of messy, but as we got more involved with our game, we started listening more attentively, wanting to be more accurate with our responses, and echo the exact same note, with a set of vowels and consonants to match the sound of rock-hitting-water.

Gaby would throw another rock, listen, and go "Ploook!" Then another rock, listen and go "Flik" for a higher note. And on and on, each rock making a different sound, going "Claak! . . . Pang!" . . . and even "Om!"

"I guess the sounding depends on how big the rock is," I tried to explain, "and also how far you throw it."

But Gaby was not interested in theory. He was too absorbed by his new experience. He was discovering the sensitivity of his hearing, his ability to hear many distinct sounds, and his talent for making all kinds of sounds and even making music. I joined in, and we were jamming with the rocks and the lake. That was really, really FUN! We called it the "Ploook Game" and came back several times to play with Lake Temescal.

Recently, scientists had discovered that kids needed to play outdoors in nature. There was a whole movement they called "leave no child inside." Time spent in nature was essential for the physical, mental, and emotional health of kids, they affirmed. They spoke about the two nervous systems involved.

The sympathetic nervous system, which is target-focused, becomes engaged during activities like using a computer, and is constantly stimulated indoors, but the parasympathetic nervous system, which is field-focused, engages when all the senses are more open, and that happens outdoors.

What's important for kids is to be able to move their attention fluidly between both target and field. That's what Gaby was doing by the lake, focusing on the stone, and then looking out to the lake and expanding his vision, going back and forth between target and field.

Kids who never go outdoors are constantly target-focused, researchers found. They lack adaptability and may end up suffering from attention-deficit disorder. But taking kids outside for unstructured play helps develop their ability to field-focus. Playing in a natural setting takes advantage of kids' natural curiosity, and it engages their whole nervous systems.

I was fortunate to have been raised by a nanny who was obsessed with fresh air, so rain or shine, we were outdoors every afternoon. For my first five years, before the war, we lived in Paris close to the Bois de Boulogne, a huge park, twice as big as Central Park, which is considered the "lungs of Paris."

My love of nature was awakened in those formative years, and later in Normandy, during the occupation, when we lived in a tiny village surrounded by farms and woods, where I could be outdoors on my own like the local kids. To this day I am obsessed, like my nanny, with the need for the outdoors, fresh air, and open space.

I was glad to pass this on to Gaby. He definitely was game, always responding with joy and creativity to our outdoor adventures.

Chapter 15

Playful Sunday with Gaby

It was one of those Saturday evenings I saved for contemplation. From my upstairs window, I watched the sunset shine on my portion of the Bay view, between the tall cedar tree and the roof of my next door neighbor. I let my eyes rest and linger in the twilight sky, humming the old popular song: "*l'heure exquise, qui nous grise lentement, la caresse, la tendresse du moment*" (the exquisite hour slowly intoxicating, the caress, the tenderness of the moment). Then I came downstairs, lit candles, burned some incense, put on some Indian music, and lay on a soft blanket on my floor, letting my body pulse, wave, and melt to the melancholic mood of the raga, knowing tomorrow was Sunday, "unassigned time," as a friend put it, time to let imagination, reverie, dreams, and feelings expand, indulging in the ease of being.

I did not turn the ringer off, just in case Gaby might call. If he called I did not want to miss him, even if it was during my meditative moments.

Gaby called and went straight to the point: "Didi, can you pick me up tomorrow?"

"Gaby . . . what's up?" I asked, startled.

"Can you pick me up tomorrow?" He was very eager to find out.

"Yes," I reassured him, "but tell me, what's going on?"

"I don't want to go with my dad and my brother; it's too boring."

"OK, and where are they going?"

"To the baseball game. Can you pick me up at ten?"

"Ten on Sunday morning, isn't that early for you all?" But I then remembered that Gaby was always the first one up.

It was Labor Day weekend, Dad's week with his sons. The parents had divorced three years back and the boys had been living one week with Mom and the next with Dad. It had been very hard for Gaby, but at least he always had his big brother Zak with him, the two of them going back and forth together between the two homes. Zak and Dad were going to watch sports all day. Gaby had tried it the year before, wanting to be with the big boys, but was not going to do this again.

"OK, I'll come at ten."

When I arrived, Gaby, now six years old, opened the door with his backpack on, ready to go. I was once again touched by the beauty of his face, his golden hair and golden skin, wide-open green eyes, happy to see me, trusting and excited.

"I want to go to the Little Farm," he launched in. "Do you have lettuce? I want to feed the cows."

"You want to feed the cows," I echoed. "Lucky cows!"

I watched how absorbed Gaby got with the two cows. He knew their names, Tiny, the big black and white one, and Sweet Pea, the brown one.

I never called cows by their names, never even imagined cows could have names, living next to the farm in Normandy where I spent part of my childhood. To me cows were cattle. They grazed all day in the fields and were guided back to the cowsheds in the evenings. I stared at the milking done by hand, even learned to do it, drank hot milk from the pail straight out of the udders, and watched how churning cream made butter. Gaby had a different concept of cows, I mused, cows as pets! I never had pets, I realized.

Sweet Pea was Gaby's favorite. She came to him. She looked enormous next to his six-year-old body. I squatted next to him to see what he saw. Her huge head was exactly at the level of his smaller head. They were face-to-face, very close, only a narrow wooden bar between them. For a second he was taken aback. She extended her tongue, as long and big as his arm, reaching for the lettuce in Gaby's hand, and kept reaching for more. Gaby got into a teasing game with her. They were both having fun. Sweet Pea looked like she was laughing with Gaby.

"*La vache qui rit!*" I exclaimed. "There she is, it's not just a cheese brand, she is real, a real laughing cow."

"*La vache qui rit*," Gaby repeated, bursting out laughing, knowing exactly what I meant. He had often made me buy the small triangular French cheese called *La vache qui rit*. He started singing: "*La vache qui rit, la vache qui rit*," to Sweet Pea's face.

Gaby could transform any event into a game and a song.

When he was done with Sweet Pea, he told her, "I am not scared of you," and moved on, proud of himself. Then he moved to the pigsty, where a new pig had arrived.

"The shed was empty for a whole year," he told me, and went on reporting all over again the drama in his most indignant voice. "Do you know that some people stole the pigs last year, the two pigs, they stole them at night, and when the ranger came in the morning, he could not find the pigs anywhere."

"Yes," I responded, "I know, I wonder what these people did with the pigs. Why do you think they stole the pigs?"

"Do you know what the ranger said?" said Gaby, outraged. "He said that they cooked the pigs for their dinner."

"I wonder how the ranger found out?" I mused.

"He did not really know," Gaby reassured me, "he just guessed." I noticed how seriously Gaby was feeling about this! It had been on his mind for a while and he was still concerned, even upset about it, and he added: "Now the ranger locks the pig at night, indoors, in his indoors shed, and no one is going to touch this pig."

It was as if he was telling me something about himself and exorcising it. There had been plenty of talk recently about little kids being kidnapped and disappearing from the streets. He had heard this, and it was not going to happen to him, he was telling me.

"OK," I confirmed, "that is NOT going to happen ever again to any pig or anyone else. Now we know how to protect them."

"Yes," echoed Gaby talking to the pig, "nobody is going to touch you, you can be sure of that."

And then we ran down the hill back to the car, Gaby yelling, "Let's go to your house."

"Time for lunch. I have cooked brown rice and salmon," I told him.

I said salmon, pronouncing the L, one of my habitual language mistakes. Gaby corrected me. "Not salllmon, *sammon*," he repeated. "Sammon, can't you say sammon?"

I repeated correctly and noticed again how much Gaby loved to teach me. We both changed roles. He was being taught all day at school, but now it was he who could teach me something, and he liked the power.

Yes, Gaby, go, Gaby, be my teacher, it's good for me, I am learning how to play, I told myself, that's exactly what I need.

We sat on the deck to eat our salmon, but soon one bee was hovering around our food. Gaby was disturbed.

"Oh, just ignore them and they'll ignore you," I told him.

"How do you ignore?" Gaby asked, irritated.

"You don't pay attention, you don't play with them, you don't fight with them, you pretend they don't exist," I replied flippantly.

This was a new game for Gaby; he was willing to try it and went on repeating, "Ignore, ignore, ignore," like a mantra that was going to dispel the problem, and he kept chanting it while I went back to the kitchen.

Soon Gaby yelled at me triumphantly, "Didi, I just ignored one and it went away."

Next we were going to play the spider game. Gaby had three orange plastic spiders, and I had three green ones, and we were going to have a fight on the plastic spider web. I started reading the instructions, but Gaby stopped me. He wanted to teach me the game himself.

That was something else he could teach me. It turned out to be the best part of the game, Gaby playing teacher and me playing learner. I got into my role; I asked him all kinds of questions about the game. It was such a treat to see what intense pleasure he took at becoming the teacher. I thought to myself that teaching might be his destiny.

At the end of the day, I made a suggestion. "Let's go to the Berkeley Marina."

It had always been one of my favorite hangouts, a beautiful waterfront. It reminded me of the time when I was standing at the top of the Greek island of Patmos years ago, surrounded by the sparkling sea, and had told myself, "I have to make sure that I always live by the sea or the ocean." I had kept my promise.

We found a flat rock at the edge of the water where we could both sit, Gaby sitting in front of me leaning against my chest. Watching the sunset, we let ourselves get splashed by the waves crashing against the rocks. When bigger waves rolled in, I felt Gaby's body tighten, holding his breath, pressing back into me. But he felt safe enough to stay put facing the surf and I was delighted to feel his trust.

We were facing west toward the Golden Gate Bridge, watching the sun slowly set behind Mount Tamalpais. The light was softening, our eyes resting on the horizon. The big, bright, orange ball of fire was sliding down and when it was all gone, Gaby said, "Now it's nighttime."

"Not quite," I replied, "it's between night and day. We have a little more time. It's not dark yet. Let's go and look at the windsurfers come home to base line."

It was twilight, and here I was, humming again the old tune, *L'heure exquise, etc.* . . .

"What are you singing?" asked Gaby.

"It's an old French song; shall I sing it for you?"

I sang it in French and then asked him, "Did you understand?"

"I know French," he retorted.

"Well, yes you do, but this is a song, it's a little different, it's about *l'heure exquise.*"

"*L'heure exquise,*" he echoed with a perfect French accent. "I never heard that word at EB." (He meant his school, Ecole Bilingue of Berkeley).

"No, I suppose you would not use this word in kindergarten," I explained. "It's kind of poetical, for special things, exquisite things that are gentle, delicate, beautiful, like this time of day, twilight, between day and night."

This exquisite hour, this enchanting moment full of tenderness and love, said the song, and this was just how I felt, *enchantée.*

We went toward the pier. There was an upper level where we could see all around, from the hills to the Bay, the three bridges, the city lights of Berkeley, Oakland, and San Francisco, the sky east, north, south, and west, the vastness I loved. We had the deck to ourselves, and we danced with the wind, with the waves, with the cypresses, with a few stars. We danced and turned and whirled with our arms wide open, leaning against the wind. Then we walked on the pier, which stretched far out into the Bay. This was a great boardwalk, and also a fishing pier where anglers sat night and day, watching their fishing rods.

Gaby's essence

The streetlights on the pier had just turned on. They were set a few yards apart, and as we walked, we found a new game. We played with our shadows. Gaby noticed how his shadow grew bigger, then smaller, as he moved between the lights, and started directing the game : "Jump over my shadow," he called. "Catch my shadow, chase my shadow." We kept running on the pier, more and more excited, playing with our shadows, in and out of each other's shadows.

The fishing people kept holding their rods, and the lovers kept huddling in the wind shelters by the railing, and the cruising people kept cruising, all of us exhilarated by the marine air.

"Play, play, play," was Gaby's refrain. He was my teacher, my play teacher.

At the end of the day, I felt refreshed, energized, and uplifted. Whether it was about the cows or the streetlights, it was all about having fun for Gaby. Melancholy was my natural state. It had its beauty and depth, but there was also joy to be lived, and I could count on Gaby to remind me. I pondered what Khalil Gibran wrote: "Our joy is our sorrow unmasked."

Chapter 16

Zak and Gaby in Paris

For the five years after my mother's death, I made a point of returning to my mother's room, the room where she had died. I traveled to Paris during the summer, when I knew my father would be away and I would have the apartment all to myself. I arrived on *rue Vavin;* the concierge gave me the keys. I entered my mother's room delicately and opened the large window. The hot summer breeze came in, the big *marronnier* greeted me, with its long branches and large leaves that I could touch while standing on the balcony: "Welcome back!"

Since my mother died, nothing had changed in her room. Only the closet and the drawers had been emptied. The room was rarely used, except sometimes as a cloak-room when there was a family reunion. It looked like a museum room, but for me it was a healing sanctuary. What I found in this room I could find nowhere else.

I would lie down on the bed where my mother slept and died, and I would get absorbed in a life-and-death rumi-nation, our lives, our deaths. I remembered what I had told my mother on her last day: you gave me my life, and now you are giving me your death. I felt the need to keep dwelling on this and there was no better place to do so. I was far away from my busy Berkeley life. Paris was half empty and quiet.

It's so strange, I thought, that this is where I become most aware of my aliveness. I feel the vibrancy of my life force, the life force all around me, the big tree outside, the sky, the birds, the city sounds in the distance, the voices coming from the backyard, the colors of the curtains, the photos on the walls, all so alive. I am enveloped by breath, spirit, soul, here in this room where my mother left her body.

"She left her body"—that's how I told it to myself, and I wondered what it meant. Did it mean that she was still something, somewhere? And who was that something? I did not have answers. I did have a rendezvous with my mother, here in her bedroom, and I loved dwelling in the mystery.

I had kept vigil over my mother's dead body. I made sure her body would not be moved for three days and three nights to allow for the slow separation between body and soul. I wanted to allow my mother's soul to leave her body gently.

I was the only one to watch over her. I was the only one to be at peace with her. My siblings had remained distant. I knew my mother had left feeling content and transformed. It happened at the last minute and for a short moment, but it did happen, and that's what counted. After our last words, my mother was ready to leave her body and I was ready to let her go. That's how I felt in this room, filled with a deep peace and fulfillment. I felt how the tenderness of those last moments with her had healed my heart. Waves of sweetness kept rippling inside my chest, and here on her bed I let myself indulge in this warm fluid wash of love. It reminded me of what Dr. Rosen had told me about love when I was a child, how much love he kept feeling for his wife and daughter long after they died in the Holocaust.

Sometimes I was overwhelmed by waves of sadness, the sadness of never having had a bond with my mother until just a few weeks before she died, the sadness of losing my mother when I had found her, the sadness of having rejected her for so long, the sadness of having rejected motherhood because I was never going to be like my mother, never going to have children.

And also I felt the sadness of rejecting myself for almost fifty years. Of her six children, I was the one most like my mother, the same body, same hands and feet, same hips, breasts, same skin, same eyes, same features. My mother and I had a lot of genes in common. Rejecting her, I had, I realized, rejected big parts of myself.

And years of sadness and longing for a loving home. When could I feel at home? Certainly not with a mother who hated any home chores and was constantly exasperated, impatient, edgy, and would take it out on anyone around her. I never felt at home, always wanted to run away, and always did. Only reluctantly would I come back when I had to. Now, lying on my mother's bed, I could weep quietly.

And on the flip side, I could see how the lack of a real home had forced me to go out into the world and create another life for myself, and I felt grateful for the options I had that my mother never had.

My mother had finally come home to herself in this room. And now I also felt at home with her, here in her room, with my memories, my insights, my sadness, my aliveness, and my companion, the big *marronnier*. Was that why I kept coming back? I could finally have a home here in Paris where I had always longed for one. I was healing my homeless heart.

When Gaby's father, Jeremy, told me he was planning to visit his brother Joel in Vienna with Zak and Gaby, I jumped on the chance to invite them to spend a few days in Paris. They would come in August when the apartment was available. By then both boys spoke fluent French, having gone to the Ecole Bilingue, and I was excited to hear them speak French in France.

I picked up Jeremy, Zak, and Gaby at the Charles de Gaulle airport. One hour later we were on the *rue Vavin*. After unloading the car and taking the bags to the lobby, we called *l'ascenseur* (the elevator). We were going to the fourth floor. This old-fashioned elevator was minuscule. Once the bags were packed in, only two bodies could squeeze inside.

The apartment building was one of those constructed before elevators existed. The staircase, going up to the sixth floor, rose smoothly, making it as pleasant a walking ascension as possible with its elegant architecture, lush red carpet on the steps, Persian rugs on the landings, and decorated light fixtures and balusters.

When elevators were invented, everybody wanted one, but where to put them was the question. The vertical shaft around which the staircase wound up was the only possible space. The size of that central space would determine the size of the elevator cab. Some cabs were smaller than others.

This one on *rue Vavin* was a really small one, mostly made of glass, with windowpanes framed by mahogany panels, and no roof. The cab ran up and down inside a see- through cage made of intricate wrought iron lace. Once in the lift, one could view the staircase as one ascended or descended.

When Gaby took his first ride up with me, I saw him staring out on all sides, very intrigued and excited. Meanwhile Zak decided to walk up, checking how fast the elevator was rising, wanting to arrive before us.

That's how Gaby and Zak invented a new game called "competing with the elevator." They would ride down together, Gaby would stay in the lift and Zak would go, "Gaby, I'll race you!"

At first they arrived on the fourth floor at the same time, no winner. That did not sit well with Zak, who was already a fiercely competitive athlete. So they started all over again. They rode back down. Gaby rode up, watching Zak run up. This time Zak managed to arrive first. It was the perfect exercise for Zak after twelve hours on the plane. And it turned out to be very exciting for both of them. Then Zak wanted to see if he could run down faster than the lift descended. That was easy; the lift went down as slowly as it went up.

This was their first experience of a different culture. They had never seen anything like it; elevators for them were boring square boxes. This was a toy, a gadget, more like a roller coaster at Disneyland. Gaby gave it a name: "the inky-dinky elevator!"

The next day they were ready for more elevator fun and begged me to let them play with it. I wondered if it was

OK. The building seemed to be empty, August in Paris. I checked with the concierge, whom I had known for years.

"*Ils sont tous partis en vacances*" (They are all gone on vacation), she said about the other tenants. "I was all alone until you arrived," she sighed. "I am glad you are here, I don't like an empty building," she added.

"And are you still working at the store next door?" I asked.

"Oh yes," she replied, "there is no vacation for people like us."

In that case, I thought, whenever she is out, from nine A.M. to five P.M., I can let Gaby and Zak play with their new toy. It won't disturb anyone. I was fascinated by the boys' creativity. They had found a new way of racing with one another! I loved their playfulness and how they brought fresh energy to old routines and institutions. They are giving me new eyes. It was the first time I really saw the exquisite design of this elevator and realized its magic.

I chose to give my mother's room to the boys. Zak, by then eight years old, would have my mother's bed, being the eldest, big and tall. For Gaby, five years old, I pulled out the futon I had slept on, and placed it between the bed and the window, exactly where I had spent the last nights with my mother. Jeremy would have my father's room. I would sleep on the dining room sofa bed.

When Gaby lay down on his futon bed for the first time, I told him to look up. He saw the big *marronnier* pouring its branches on top of him through the big French window and asked me, "What's that?"

"That's the top of a tree," I laughed.

Gaby had never seen the crown of a full-grown tree. In Berkeley most of us live under the trees. "*Les voyages forment la jeunesse*" (traveling shapes youth), I thought.

Chapter 17

Gaby, Maillot Jaune

For the weekend, the four of us, Jeremy, the boys, and I, got in the car and drove to Chatillon, a village one hour south of Paris, where my brother lived with his wife and three kids in a big old family mansion. The back yard, in typical classical French design, was more like a small park, with a large round lawn at the center, surrounded by a ring of well-kept lanes for evening walks, bordered by ancient trees giving thick shade in this hot summer month. At the back was an abandoned tennis court.

In the garage were many bikes of different sizes. Everyone, my brother and his seven-year-old son Antoine, Jeremy and Zak, Gaby and I, all found a bike our size. They decided to take off on a long tour of the nearby Loire châteaux. I had seen enough castles for the rest of my life and decided to stay back with Gaby and bike around the estate.

After having gone on three wheels for a while, Gaby had just become a two-wheeler before leaving Berkeley and was so proud of it, he had to tell everybody he met: "Guess what, I am a two-wheeler!" he proclaimed.

Yes, achievements that made him feel like the other kids were important.

After adjusting the seats, Gaby and I got on our bikes. First I led the way, trying out all the alleys of the park, gently curving into one another. Then Gaby led the way. The bikes were fine. We had the whole afternoon. I felt like the eight-year-old I once was, riding all over the countryside in Normandy, on my *bicyclette*, a free spirit.

Suddenly I transformed into a cycling coach with surprising authority. I remembered Tony, a man I had had an affair with in Boulder, Colorado in the seventies. Tony was one of the cycling coaches for the American Olympic team. Several times I followed Tony and his bikers, and from my car I could watch him function in his coach capacity. I was curious to discover the world of competitive athletes, fascinated by the extreme energy put out by the coach.

Here, after so many years, I found myself becoming Tony. I was amazed how much I had internalized Tony's role and how I could impersonate him. I would ride behind Gaby and egg him on, calling instructions in my most bossy voice: "Slow down, lean right . . . Lean left, breathe . . . Faster, watch the curve, slow down, prepare to stop . . . Start, breathe, use your right leg, keep going. . . . Breathe, focus on your right leg," on and on, getting excited myself.

The main circular alley became our racing track. We kept going around and around, gaining momentum, learning how to lean toward the center of the circle as it curved, and then reversing the direction and building up speed again.

I noticed how Gaby went faster when his right leg, the weaker one, was on the inside of the ring and when his left leg, much stronger, was pedaling on the outside. Of course Gaby wanted to keep going in the same direction all the time, but I was not going to let him get away with this, and made him bike two rounds with right leg outside for each round with left leg outside, teaching him, "Gaby, it's not only about speed, it's about getting stronger and working the weaker links."

Gaby was always eager to get stronger. He was now older. He enjoyed the trainer-trainee relationship, although it was a new one for him, and rose to the challenges with enthusiasm.

After working the main track, we got into the side alleys and had to manage shorter curves and turns. Gaby, getting bolder and bolder, fell off his bike a few times, but the ground was soft, moist dirt. He didn't care. He was fired up.

After taking a break and drinking a lot of water, we moved to the old tennis court, covered with asphalt, a smaller and harder ground, with the net raised. I showed Gaby a new challenging practice: making figure eights from one end of the court to the other end, sliding his head down under the net. It was easy for me to demonstrate, but for Gaby it was not so much fun at first. He resisted it, but I kept cheerleading, and when he managed to do it, he knew he had mastered something really big. I was a proud coach, taking his training seriously and showing him his potential.

When Gaby reached his top performance at the end of the day, we did a slowing-down phase before quitting and I congratulated him as a satisfied coach would do: "*Félicitations, Gaby, bon travail! Maillot jaune!*"

Everyone in France knows what *maillot jaune* means: it's the yellow shirt worn by the winner of the Tour de France.

The next morning, I drove early to the closest town

to buy a yellow T-shirt for Gaby. "*Voilà, le maillot jaune pour Gaby,*" I announced, presenting it to him in front of the whole applauding family.

Gaby, wearing his new T-shirt, got back on his bike and went racing around the center lawn, pressing his thumb on the bell, *gling, gling, gling,* and shouting in French, "*Attention, voilà le maillot jaune qui passe!*" (Watch out, here is the yellow shirt!)

Chapter 18

Low Tide at Agate Beach, Bolinas

I was in love with Bolinas long before I arrived in the Bay Area. In the sixties, hippie travelers from California whom I met on the road, in Spain or India, spoke of Bolinas as a magical Mecca, sitting at the edge of the American continent, the tip end of the Western world.

After settling in Berkeley, I was dreaming of having a week-end home in Bolinas.

Bolinas is a small village in the most remarkable natural setting, off the beaten path, hidden, quaint. Many people who come here are self-sufficient, naturalists, conservationists, artists, poets, musicians, dancers. I wanted to feel part of this community.

My search took me to Simona, who owned a house perched on the bluff, the Little Mesa, overlooking Bolinas village on one side and the lagoon on the other, surrounded by a grove of tall eucalyptus trees. A hippie dancer and feminist, Simona had designed her house with music-and-dance workshops in mind, a vast room with high ceiling and wooden floor, and two small rooms up on the mezzanine.

Simona and I figured out a good arrangement. She stayed in my Berkeley home, tending to her urban needs, while I stayed in her Bolinas house, trading long weekends or just overnights.

Being on a peninsula, Bolinas had beaches on three sides; Agate Beach was one of them, an exceptional seascape, one of the best places to see tidal pools at low tides. I kept track of the tides. Every January, I bought the new tide schedule for the year. I would look for days, preferably on weekends, when the tides were going to be at their lowest. I saved those days, favorite beach days. The wet sand was hard and the terrain good for dancing, feet in bubbles of foam at the tip of the waves. I had practiced this form of outdoor movement meditation for a long time on many different beaches, in the south of France, India, Spain, Bali, beaches in Maine, the Carolinas, and now California. And when the tide pools were exposed, the teeming sea life was fun to explore.

Now in this month of May, it all came together. Simona was away, her house was available, the tide was very low at eleven A.M. on a Saturday, and Gaby was up for an overnight adventure. I was going to initiate him into the wonders of Agate Beach.

When I picked him up in the morning, Gaby was ready to go, with his backpack, his small suitcase and his new pet, Fluffy the polar bear.

The ride to Bolinas was gorgeous. The road wound up Mount Tamalpais through a thick forest of huge pine trees and redwoods, and then suddenly we were on the other side, out in the open and facing the spectacular view of the shoreline and the Pacific Ocean.

I stopped the car for a moment to take in the clear sky, the soft morning light, the blue ocean. "Look, Gaby, look, Stinson Beach down there, where you went swimming last summer.

And a little further, do you see the big lagoon, and that small hill at the tip end of the beach? That's where we are going."

"Awesome, it's awesome!" Gaby assessed.

"Yes, that's the right word, it IS awesome!" I confirmed. "Awesome like unique, and magnificent, and breathtaking."

When we arrived at the house, we found the key to the gate in its usual hidden spot. Gaby fell in love with the garden; it was overgrown with yellow and purple lupines in full bloom, as high as his chest. We called it our "secret garden," like the movie we had watched together recently. It was fenced in on all sides, protected and very intimate. In the center was the fire pit, circled with several big stones.

"Let's have a fire and tell stories," Gaby said excitedly.

"Good idea," I agreed, "later we could do that."

We went around the house. Here was a collection of drums from around the world, congas, doumbeks, tars, mridangas, tablas, and other instruments like the mbira and the xylophone.

"Cool, cool," Gaby declared each time he picked one up and played with it. He was familiar with musical instruments, but some of these were new to him.

When it was time to prepare dinner, Gaby cooked his own tofu. He put a little oil in a small pan, grabbed the whole chunk of tofu out of its box with one hand, let it slide into the pan, and watched it sizzle. He ate it plain.

"That's all you're going to eat?" I asked, munching on my rice and kale.

"Yes," he said, "it's SO good."

The sun was going down, the kitchen was bathed in

golden light. I said casually, "Golden light for a golden boy," which he echoed turning it into a song.

"Golden light for a golden boy."

We kept singing, in call-and-response mode.

"Where is the golden boy?" I called.

"Running down the hill, catching the golden light," he responded.

"Did the golden boy catch the golden light?" I called.

"Yes he did, yes he did, yes he did," he responded, getting carried away, like singing gospel.

"Yes he did, yes, he did, yes he did."

Gaby was off and running around the garden, around the small trails between the tall flowers, his bright blond hair catching the last golden rays. Gaby was a musician in his genes. He had been learning musical comedy songs for several years already with his grandmother, a voice teacher and chorus director.

The time had come to prepare our bonfire.

"I am going to get a lot of this bark and make a pile of it," he announced as he gathered stuff fallen from the eucalyptus trees.

"OK, I am going to bring more wood from the indoor fireplace," I added.

We struck a few matches, and there went the flames. We sat on the big stones and welcomed Fire with music and songs. Gaby played the tambourine; I had the doumbek. We were jamming. I opened the session, addressing the fire itself: "We give thanks to you, great Fire; warm our bodies, warm our hearts, light up our spirits!"

Then Gaby got into his song. "When people ask me what will I be when I am a grownup, I say, maybe I'll be the sky, maybe a bike, or maybe I'll be a child, for the rest of my life."

I became the chorus and repeated the refrain: "Maybe I'll be a child for the rest of my life," totally enjoying the idea. Sure, I was the grownup, but I was also a child when I was Gaby's playmate. It's as if I were his big sister playing with my little brother. When Gaby told me, "I am your brother" years ago, I could have answered, "Yes, and I am your big sister." We were two kids, lighthearted, free spirits. I told myself, "It's never too late to have a happy childhood," realizing how that worn-out cliché was really true for me.

When the fire died down, we shared the big bed. Gaby slept until seven thirty the next morning, deep sound sleep, safe and secure holding his Fluffy, while I watched over him, staying up as if I needed to protect him. My sleep was worried and shallow and I was sad to realize that I was still haunted by the irrational fear of losing a child if I fell asleep.

Our big day at Agate Beach had come. We packed our picnic and our water shoes.

Agate Beach is named for the millions of tiny agate pebbles brought in by the rolling surf. We walked to the end of the beach where a huge eucalyptus tree fell years ago, uprooted from the towering cliffs by some wild storm. The thick trunk and naked branches were polished and smoothed, like driftwood, by the relentless crashing waves. This was our home base.

The tide was as low as it was going to be. The famous Duxbury Reef, the largest shale reef in North America, was exposed. It looked like gray pumice, probably a remnant of volcanic eruptions.

An older man was already wandering around, scrutinizing the pools. Gaby, stepping cautiously on the rocks, across the little rivers as he called them, went toward him and asked shyly, "What are you looking for?"

"Good question," answered the man, who turned out to be a marine biologist and teacher, as I learned later, and seemed only too happy to explain everything to Gaby.

I stayed on the sand, dancing to the sounds and movements around me, to the deep ocean roar, the squeaking seagulls, the gliding pelicans, the breeze in the clouds, and the flights of so many birds. I was filled with the ocean air, with the smells, the sun, the sea spray, getting ozone high.

I saw Gaby and his new friend over there squatting, looking intently, the old expert and his new acolyte, poking and probing in the pools. They were a good match. I was always fascinated how Gaby would, quietly and gently, attach himself to someone he had just met and follow him or her around for a while. People did not seem annoyed. On the contrary, they seemed touched and delighted. He was so curious and open to learning, and at the same time he gave back something from his heart, his joie de vivre and his tenderness.

I never found out what the teacher was really doing there; maybe he was the tide pools' angel. When they were done, he said good-bye and walked away.

Now Gaby had a new passion for marine life and wanted to show it off. He took me around the pools and introduced me to the marine creatures he had just met, switching roles, becoming the teacher while I played student. Each time we played this game, I felt rejuvenated. It was as if I turned into Gaby for a few minutes.

After our lunch picnic, Gaby got me to play monkeys all over the great fallen tree, climbing the branches, balancing on the narrow ones, hanging from the high ones, fun and safe with the soft warm sand as our safety net.

Then Gaby spotted a fisherman standing knee-deep in the waves at the other end of the beach. "Let's go see what he is doing."

"You go," I suggested, "I am holding the fort."

I saw Gaby approach the fisherman. That's another strategy of his. He got close, he stared, and he waited until he was invited.

A Vietnamese family was on the beach, maybe twelve of them. The old man was fishing and he had already caught several perch and five crabs. The women were sitting around, preparing the fire to barbecue the catch, like in the old country. A bunch of little kids were running toward Gaby. I enjoyed watching the kids, their freedom to come and go, to seize the moment, sharing their excitement.

They got Gaby to play with them at throwing stones in the water, skipping rocks.

Soon Gaby was adopted by the family. From our base camp by the fallen tree, I saw him sitting with them, all eating watermelon together.

I waved to him, making signs. "Soon we must leave. The tide is coming in."

"Let's play, let's not waste time," screamed Gaby, laughing and running away with his new gang.

Eventually the Vietnamese family was packing up, preparing to leave as well. When the tide was high, there was hardly any beach left, and nobody wanted to be trapped against the cliffs.

I caught up with Gaby. On our way back to the car, the family gave him a watermelon, a small one but a whole one. That really impressed Gaby.

"A whole watermelon!" He kept telling me, "They gave me a WHOLE watermelon," and he broke into a song. "The whole one, with the whole family, the whole ocean, the whole sky, the whole day, the whole world," and since he knew the classic gospel, he crescendoed, "in his hands, he's got the whole world. He's got the whole whole whole world."

He could not seem to get enough of this word WHOLE, as if the word itself had a magical power which gave him a deep satisfaction, almost a healing, I told myself, as I realized how broken his family had been, and his longing for what he lost at three when his mother left for a month and his parents divorced.

"In his hands he's got the whole world."

"Yes, Gaby," I affirmed, "and who's this guy who's got the whole world?" I asked, impishly.

"You know who he is," he replied, "He's got the whole world! That's who he is!"

I felt proud of his answer.

At the end of the day, driving back to Berkeley, we stopped by the lagoon, home of the great blue herons and the white egrets.

"Look, Gaby, it's feeding time; they are busy looking for their dinner."

"Dinner time, dinner time, dinner time," Gaby chanted.

Back up the mountain, we stopped the car where we had stopped the day before. The sun was now setting bright orange on the ocean horizon, a vast and quiet peace in front of us. Gaby recognized the sites and now he was the one saying back to me, "Look, Didi, look! Stinson Beach, and the lagoon, and all the way out there," he added with a burst of excitement, almost screaming, "it's Bolinas!"

Bolinas, here was a great-sounding word, full of vocal fun for Gaby. He came up with a celebration song, conducting me. "You sing the chorus," he told me, "just repeat *at Bolinas* after me, each time I tell you."

"That was a happy day . . . *at Bolinas*

"That was a lucky day . . . *at Bolinas*

"That was a sunny day . . . *at Bolinas*

"That was a friendly day . . . *at Bolinas.*"

I kept driving and we kept singing about special moments experienced *at Bolinas.* And that was the end of our journey to the end of the Western world.

I was showing Gaby his country. We were both new to this beautiful land, he as a child and I as an expat. I was sharing with him my passion for the great outdoors, which, like a powerful lover, kept drawing me back and keeping me entranced. I was telling Gaby how fortunate we were to have the mountain, the forest, the ocean, the shore so close to our Berkeley home. "We will be back soon," I assured him.

Chapter 19

Full Moon Gazing in Bali

"Live with a full moon in each eye."—*Hafiz*

When I joined the hippie tribe in Spain, I adopted their pagan celebrations. In Formentera, this smallest island of the Baleares, the full moon nights were magical events. We stayed up all night on the beach, swimming in the moon's soft silvery light, in and out of the gentle waves, getting high, and dancing to live music until dawn.

My first night in India was also magical. The plane landed around midnight. I walked out of the sordid airport by myself, instantly assailed by taxi drivers, but when I looked at the sky and saw the brightest full moon, I relaxed in the warm tropical night.

A clunky taxi took me to Malabar Hill, an elegant neighborhood of Bombay, and dropped me in front of a deluxe apartment building. There was even a doorman who opened the elevator door, took me to the eighth floor, and rang the bell. Although it was late, a woman's face with a huge smile invited me in. She was Lalita, Margarita's friend, and knew I was coming. She immediately led me to the balcony, where I exclaimed, "You can see everything—the city, the ocean, the sky, and the full moon! What a clear night! What an awesome sight!"

"Yes," she agreed, "this is the highest floor in the highest building on the highest hill in Bombay, and the full moon in May is always the most brilliant of all. I was sitting here enjoying it. Come, let's sit together." Soon she added, "Landing for the first time in India on a full moon night is very auspicious." She explained, "I will call you Purnima. It will be your Indian name."

"Purnima," I repeated, trying out how it sounded. "What does it mean?"

"Purnima is a common name given to girls, it means full moon."

Since no one knew my French name yet, I became Purnima, Full Moon, for the next ten years. From then on, I would be looking for the moon every night and learning about her phases and schedules, how she rises and sets opposite to the sun. Even my monthly periods were following the moon's cycles. This gave me a connection to the cosmos, the sky, the night, the infinite. I lived in the expectation of the full moon, waiting to celebrate her fullness every month.

During the five years I lived in India, I had plenty of special full moon celebrations. The most meaningful moment for me was the instant she appeared over the horizon. I figured out exactly where she was going to rise, and I was ready at the right time, and at the right place, to witness her apparition as she slowly rose.

The best visions I had were in Pondicherry, where I lived at the Aurobindo Ashram for one year, on the southern Bay of Bengal coast, where the full moon emerged out of the ocean. I was her lady-in-waiting, ready on the beach or on the roof of my bungalow, to greet her and dance for joy.

When I moved to Berkeley, I found out that close to my new home was the perfect spot to rendezvous with the full moon: Inspiration Point at the top of Tilden Park, away from all streetlights, where I could see the moon rise over the distant horizon.

This is where I took Gaby for our next adventure, his initiation to the full moon rising. He was ten years old. Parking at twilight, we took off on the long crest trail. After walking for twenty minutes, we reached the first bench facing east, where the sky was immense.

"This is where we are going to see the full moon rise, just over that hill, to the right of Mount Diablo," I told Gaby. "Let's sit and wait for her to appear."

"How long are we going to wait?" Gaby asked.

"Not long at all. I always check online what time the moon rises over the horizon, and then I add about twenty minutes for her to show up over the hills. It should be very soon," I explained.

"We are just going to sit here and stare at the sky?" Gaby was puzzled.

"Yes, exactly, and if you look well, you can already see the sky becoming lighter over there. That's where she is going to come from, and if you keep staring you'll see a dot of bright light."

"I see it," Gaby exclaimed, "I see a small bright light. Is that the moon?"

"Yes, here she is, see, the dot is getting bigger already," I confirmed.

"Oh, she is rising in the sky . . . she is rising in the sky . . . she is getting almost round . . . she is getting fat . . . now she is all round . . . Wow! In slo-mo!" Gaby, getting very excited, stood right up with arms stretched up to the sky.

"And did you know the moon could be bright orange like this?" I asked. "That's because she is catching the last rays of the sun setting over there on the other side, and when the sun is all set, she will become all white."

Gaby and I sat a little longer, illumined by the orange moon, watching her floating herself up. We kept quiet for a moment. Then I asked, "Hey Gaby, do you want to hear the story of the full moon and the piglets?"

"OK."

"You remember when I went to Bali last year?"

"Yes, I know, you sent me a postcard."

"Well, I was at a very strange full moon festival. It happens only once a year on the October full moon. We got a ride, Lou and I, to this remote village. At the end of a long bumpy road, the driver stopped the minivan at the foot of a mountain. We were suddenly surrounded by so many people we could hardly get out of the Bemo. Men all in white, women in golden dresses, lots of kids in bright costumes. The crowd was going up a very steep stone stairway, straight up the mountain. We followed them. The steps were high and filled with people, like on the train at rush hour. The men and women were carrying something on their heads." I paused.

"What? What did they carry?" Gaby was getting impatient.

"Each of them carried on their head a baby pig, yes, a piglet, set on a big tray, imagine, a whole piglet on their head."

"A real one?" exclaimed Gaby.

"Yes, a real one, but not alive. It was cooked, roasted, glazed, and even decorated with flowers, marigolds all around the piglet on the tray. They were carrying them to the top of the mountain. They had raised their own pigs in their backyards. They made sure one new baby pig was going to be ready for that very special festival."

"Why did they do that?" Gaby frowned.

"Well, we had no idea until we got to the top. The climb was hard. It seemed to go on forever. It was exhausting, but the people were so cheerful, chatting and laughing, that we kept going. We did not understand their language, but we kept climbing with everyone else. I was following Lou, my American friend who lives in Bali. He was a very tall blond man, taller than everyone else, which helped, so I did not lose him in the crowd. Finally we got to the top. And you know what we saw? All the piglets on their trays were placed on a large altar, in the moonlight, offered to the moon, many, many dishes of roasted piglets, surrounded by scores of burning incense sticks. The piglets in Bali are considered to be the most delicious food. They are cooked with the most fragrant spices, only the best for the full moon."

"But how can the moon eat the piglets? This is a crazy story," Gaby declared.

"Yes, I know it sounds crazy, but wait. After leaving their offerings, the people sat on the other side of the mountain facing the ocean. The view was fabulous. The ocean was shining like a huge mirror reflecting the silver moonlight, and you know what they were doing?"

"What?"

"Gazing at the moon. So we sat on the ground too, and gazed at the moon, at the sky, at the ocean. People had come all the way to the top of the mountain so that they could be closer to the moon and sit with her as she was slowly descending toward the ocean. They came to spend the night with the full moon, to offer her their very best food and to sit with her. There were hundreds of people all seated on the ground huddled together. From the top of the mountain down to the ocean, the slope was filled with people. Can you imagine if this slope here was filled with people, what that would be like?"

"How long did they sit there?" asked Gaby.

"They were going to keep company to the moon all night until she set in the ocean."

"They just sat there doing nothing? And what happened to the piglets?"

"I was sitting on the ground next to a young woman who sang a sweet melody over and over again. I asked her about it. She giggled. She did not understand English, nor did anyone else near us, but she pointed to the moon. She was serenading the moon, I guessed. Other people were also chanting softly and it all seemed to blend perfectly. It made a beautiful humming sound rising from the crowd."

"Did you sing too?"

"I hummed along. I thought, this is the most beautiful full moon of my life, I will never forget it."

"But what happened to the piglets?" Gaby kept asking.

"Some time later, clouds arrived and the moon disappeared. Moon gazing time was over. People started getting up, very slowly and quietly walking back to the altar where the piglets had been placed. The Prasad started. Lots of men, all in white like high priests, broke off the piglets with their hands, and gave out Prasad. First the children received a good piece of meat in their open hands, then the adults. Everyone kept bowing to the moon as they relished their piece of piglet, because it was the gift of the moon. The Prasad of the full moon."

"What kind of word is that, 'Prasad'?" asked Gaby, pronouncing it perfectly.

"It's a very common word in Bali and India. It means 'food that has been blessed.' The piglets had been offered to the moon and blessed by the moon, and the moon was returning the piglets to her devotees for them to eat and enjoy."

"Did you eat some piglet?" Gaby asked.

"Oh yes, I had a good piece of full moon piglet. An older woman put it in my hands, and another big piece in Lou's hands. And I bowed to the moon for her Prasad. It was sticky, juicy, and delicious. You would have loved it.

"Then it was all over. The crowd walked down the steep stairways, holding on to one another, because it was dark, dark clouds were hiding the moon. I held on to people too. We had become a big family, including the two of us white tourists. When we reached the bottom of the mountain, it suddenly poured just in time for us to run to our minivan. The rain was also the blessing of the full moon. That's my Bali story. Did you like it?"

Gaby thought about it and suddenly realized, "We did not offer anything to the moon."

"Yes, it's true, we came empty-handed, but at least we greeted her when she rose, we offered our company and talked about her. That's something."

"One day I will go to Bali," declared Gaby, "and while people are gazing at the moon, I will sneak to the piglets and grab one and have a whole one to myself. I bet it tastes real good. OK," he added, looking at me, "OK, I will bow to the moon with a piglet in my hand and say, 'Thank you, moon'!"

The moon was high, and Gaby was ready to go. I had managed to keep him gazing at the moon for a good half hour. On the way back, I taught Gaby a song to the moon I had learned at a Native American ritual in New Mexico:

Mother Moon, watch over me
Your child I'll always be
Mother Moon watch over me
Until I am free
Mother Moon shine down on me
I am you and you are me
And we are part of everything.

"Next time, you can sing this song with your beautiful voice and offer it to the moon," I added, concluding our ritual.

Chapter 20

I Don't Want to Lose a Second One; Hawaii

When Gaby was a baby, and until he was twelve years old, I had a recurring nightmare about losing him. There were many different variations on the same theme: Gaby was in my care and I lost him. Like this one: Gaby and I are sitting in the Paris airport, waiting. It's very crowded. I leave Gaby alone with our bags for a few minutes. When I come back, he has disappeared. I run all over the airport, yelling, "Gaby, Gaby . . . *Où es tu?* Where are you?" I am asking everyone around, "Where is the child? Where is the child? Did you see the child?" I am crazed with panic and wake up terrified.

I had also noticed that when I had Gaby in my car, I drove slower. I was always extra cautious, even anxious to prevent any possible accident.

When he was about six, Gaby was accepted at the Golden Lion Kung Fu School for little kids. I would take him to the class, stay, and watch. Kids were taught to kick and punch, excellent for body coordination. Gaby took it very seriously and was thrilled to play rough. After the class we would go to my home. Filled with energy, Gaby wanted to keep practicing his moves. To make sure that Gaby would not hurt himself, I had made a series of bolsters and cushions out of foam rubber, which I placed as buffers in front of every window, beside every piece of furniture, and at every sharp angle in the room.

Creating safe space and protecting Gaby from any possible danger was my function and my mission. I did not question this obsession at first, but eventually it came to a head.

When Gaby was twelve and he did not have to wear a day brace any more, just one at night, I invited him on a ten-day trip to Hawaii, just the two of us. He wore hightops most of the time to support his ankle, and we bought a pair of Speedo water shoes for the beach. Gaby felt very special and was ready to go.

Soon we were visiting friends, Tara, her husband, and their son Alan, who lived on a long quiet beach at Haleiwa.

Alan was sixteen, four years older than Gaby. He had spent his whole life on that beach and he was an expert at boogie boarding. Alan was going to teach Gaby. Looking at Gaby, tall and chubby, Alan could not imagine what Gaby's body had been through. Alan spent just a few minutes showing him how to ride a few small waves close to the beach. Soon Alan was surfing further and further away from the beach, and of course Gaby was following him. Tara and I were watching them from the deck of the house. They seemed to be getting very far away. For a long time, staring at them appearing and disappearing with the waves, I could feel my anxiety level rising and rising. Each time a wave would take Gaby out of sight, I froze until the next wave would bring him up again.

Tara was trying to reassure me. "Don't worry, it's safe, it's not that deep out there, it's not dangerous, they are OK."

"You know," I argued, "Gaby is weaker than he looks. You probably could not tell, but his whole right side is weaker and less coordinated than his left one. He always ignores it. He does not want other kids to know about it. But what if he found himself exhausted out there and did not have the strength to come back to shore?"

I ran down to the beach, into the water up to my knees, trying to get closer to the boys, and started yelling at Gaby to come back. Of course, he could not hear me with the sounds of the waves all around him, but I kept yelling and yelling and yelling, and gesticulating. "Come back . . . come back . . . come back," I shouted, feeling more and more anxious.

Tara kept trying to calm me down. I repeated that Gaby had no sense of his limits. I could not contain myself anymore, and, terrified of what could happen, I finally cried out, "I just don't want to lose a second one," and broke down sobbing in Tara's arms. As she held me, I told Tara in a few words about the first one I had lost when I was seven.

Alan and Gaby finally came back. Gaby was furious at me. "What's going on? What do you want? What's wrong with you?" he ranted.

"Look," I managed to explain, "you are not Alan, you are not a great swimmer, you have no experience with a boogie board, this is your first time, and you've been out for too long already. That's it! You are not going out again."

Gaby hated me for reminding him of the weakness he

kept ignoring. Tara understood I needed time, and took the boys out to dinner while I stayed back, completely undone by my panic explosion.

Waves of sobbing shook me again, shook my gut, my womb, my heart, and my whole being. Even after years of deep kundalini meditation, after many bodywork therapy sessions, and heart-healing moments with Gaby, there was still a frozen block deep inside me that had not been touched, a frozen block of dread, the dread of losing another beloved child. This block finally cracked open, and the iceberg began to thaw.

As my whole body kept shaking from jaw to knees, releasing layers of fear, I saw my whole life flashing in front of me. I noticed how I had avoided all kinds of attachments before getting attached to Gaby. I had chosen a childfree life; I had come to that decision at a very young age. Not only had I lost my baby brother then, but my mother as well: lost in her grief, her guilt, her rage, she had cut me out for good, abandoned and left with her unspoken legacy: don't be a mother, it's too painful. I understood that when I got attached to Gaby, I had taken a huge risk without knowing it.

At the time, my schoolteacher, *ma maitresse*, who was the opposite of my mother, became my role model. I knew she had no children of her own. She was cheerful and loved her job. I imagined becoming a teacher like her, or an explorer, not a family person.

After my abortion, when I was in my thirties and forties with the biological clock ticking, I had been a PhD student, then I was on the road, and then I lived in an ashram.

It was only when I was forty-five that I settled down, way past childbearing years. I had subconsciously avoided getting caught by the procreating urge.

Then something unpredictable happened; a new baby boy showed up in my life, and without the slightest hesitation, I did what I was never going to do, I got totally attached. I was not his mother, but I became his godmother and got involved with him just as if I was his mother. This attachment brought back the delight of loving and caring for a new life, but eventually would also revive the deep fear of losing him.

Tara and the boys came back. Gaby, who could never hold a grudge, was happy again. Tara pitched a small tent for him on the deck and I crashed under the stars, emotionally emptied and exhausted.

For the rest of our vacation, Gaby and I went swimming many more times at different beaches. He discovered snorkeling and forgot Boogie Boarding. I was relaxed and playful again. Something had shifted. I felt lighter. I had let go of a terrible burden. Gaby was twelve. It was time to support his need for independence. I noticed that my recurring panic nightmares had stopped.

Now that I did have a "second one" in my life, I felt ever more grateful for this second chance. I was not haunted by the fear of losing Gaby any more. I was caring for him out of my conscious choice and deep love, not out of fear. In the background, I kept hearing Kate Wolf singing, "Give yourself to love . . . Open up your heart to the tears and laughter, and give yourself to love."

Chapter 21

At the Meher Spiritual Center, Myrtle Beach, South Carolina

"Real happiness lies in making others happy."
—*Meher Baba*

That these five hundred acres were once a shooting preserve when Myrtle Beach was a small town, and that now, sixty years later, this land had become a wildlife sanctuary, was a good example of the paradoxes and jokes Meher Baba enjoyed. The closest neighbor of this ecological treasure, the sole refuge left for the native birds, animals, and plants rejected by the exploding commercial development, was now a Mega Walmart!

In 1943, this piece of land was given to Meher Baba to become his home in America, as he later described it. Of all possible places in the United States, it was the only one that fulfilled his five requests: mild climate, virgin land, fertile soil, ample fresh water, and given from the heart. Yes, it was given from the heart of one of his lifelong American disciples.

This is where I go every spring, to the Meher Center, "a Retreat for Rest, Meditation and the Renewal of Spiritual Life."

I never met Meher Baba, the great Indian spiritual Master. He had left his body in 1969, but in 1996, years after my first spiritual teacher had passed away, I went back to India on a second pilgrimage to visit Meher Baba's home and tomb. I met his lifelong companions who were still alive. The atmosphere of love and simple beauty around them was so remarkable that I came to recognize that Meher Baba was my spiritual guide, and would be for the rest of my life. I vowed to keep listening to his inner guidance and to follow his teachings.

The first time I came to the Meher Center in Myrtle Beach, I fell in love with the unique combination of ocean, dunes, wetlands and marshland, freshwater lakes and maritime forests, which created a vast bubble of stillness and silence protected by the constant humming of wildlife. This was an ideal place for meditation, for listening to the voice that is heard deep within the heart.

I walked for hours with my feet in the ocean up to my knees on the beautiful fine sand beach that extends, protected and untouched, for more than a mile. Or I sat on the deck by the long and narrow lake fed by hidden springs and gazed endlessly at the rippling waters and tall grasses, breathing in the exhilarating marine air.

It was only later that I connected with the land. I had never lived around marshes. This kind of seaside forest was unfamiliar, but one day the land revealed itself to me in the form of one special flower. I was walking back to my cabin and I almost stepped on it. I picked it up and saw the most unusual bloom, composed of five pale-green petals with a band of bright orange around its creamy center, resembling a tulip, but as thick and pulpy as some succulent leaves. It had just fallen on the trail. Where did it come from? I wondered, looking up and around and finding no clue.

That's how I learned about the tulip poplar, a magnificent tree with a very tall trunk. Its tulips bloom only high up at the very top of the tree. I would have never seen this flower had it not fallen on the path just minutes before I walked by. From then on, first thing every morning, I would go to the poplar tree and see if a flower had fallen during the night. Every time I found one was the same magic moment.

These poplars like to keep their feet and roots wet. I followed the meanderings of tiny marshy creeks hidden by layers of dead leaves that I pushed away with my boots. They took me deep into this unique seaside forest where the salt spray spreads far and wide, and during storms and hurricanes has the strangest effect on young trees. They grow into the most fascinating weird shapes.

The Center became a place where I could listen and speak not only to my inner voice but also to the many voices of the trees, to the shrubs like the buckeye plants, the wax myrtle plants, and the yaupons, to the creepers, to the squirrels, the egrets, the lonely owl, and many others.

Easter break 2001: Gaby was now fourteen and had completed his bar mitzvah. It was time to invite him to come and spend his vacation at the Meher Spiritual Center, knowing that other kids, from different parts of the country, would also be there. And as his godmother, I wanted to share with him my experiences of sacred grounds and spiritual connection to a higher power.

"I came prepared," Gaby showed me, when we met at the Oakland airport. He was dressed in black from head to toe, including a black cap pulled all the way down, and black gloves. He was hooked up to his CD player—this was before iPods—and had his CD collection handy in his black backpack. He listened either to rap music or to the Beatles. He knew the words of all these songs by heart and sang along to himself here at the airport while we waited for our flight. I guess that's what he meant by coming "prepared"; he brought his own world along.

Arriving at the Center in a rented car, we stopped at the front gate to register. Gaby was warmly welcomed. Residents and caretakers of the Center loved to see teenagers. The first thing Gaby asked, declaring his priorities, was, "Is there a basketball hoop?"

"Well, of course!" replied Jeff, the grounds manager, "and we need someone just like you on our team."

Driving down the long sandy forest trail to our cabin, I was going ten miles an hour. Gaby was getting impatient next to me. "Why do you have to drive so slowly?"

"It's a policy of the Center," I explained, "to protect the trails."

"Whatever!" snarled Gaby, sticking to his "attitude."

I parked the car and would not use it again until our departure. Unless arriving or leaving, guests were restricted to bicycles only, while the staff zipped around in golf carts.

Our cabin, called "Cabin on the Hill," had two rooms with the bathroom in between, and a large screened porch with a view of the lake. That was where we would live for the next ten days together. All the cabins were lovingly furnished with bedside lamps, rocking chairs, cushions, pillows, rugs, and photos of Meher Baba on the walls.

Gaby dropped his bags on his bed and asked right away, "So what shall we do?" He was ready for some action after all that sitting around on planes and in the car. He had slept perfectly on the plane. I was tired, but I was so happy that we were at Meher Baba's home for real that I was seized with a new energy, and we were off checking out the basketball court, then the ping-pong area, and on to the refectory to organize the food we had bought on our way from the airport.

There were no kitchens in the cabins. Visitors brought their own food and shared two common kitchens, lovely buildings under the trees with plenty of space for cooking, storing food, and dining on the porches. This was where everybody met, guests and staff alike, everybody friendly, especially to new people like Gaby. He got another big hit of welcome, especially from Jeff, who had already noticed Gaby's limp and taken him on the grand tour of the Center in his golf cart. That was the kind of attention Gaby thrived on. He had just become an important guest, and I saw his "attitude" melt away.

For the first two days, Gaby hung out with me and other adults, sharing meals with us, but by the third day, he had connected with the kids, a whole gang of them moving as a pack all over the Center, from morning till the Center's curfew at eleven P.M., free and safe. I hardly saw him again, only for a few minutes when he was hungry.

Our second night was a full moon night. I suggested the two of us go to the boathouse looking over Long Lake, to watch the moon rise. Gaby, listening to *Abbey Road* on his CD player, sat on the deck just a few inches above the water.

The night was clear, and the rising moon seemed very close to us. I was standing on the floating deck, swaying to the subtle rhythm of the rippling waters under my feet, deeply inhaling the ocean breeze. The reflection of the moon on the lake seemed to open up a timeless dimension, and as she continued to rise we kept watching her, each one of us in our own inner world. There was no one else on the deck. I was as happy as I could ever imagine being, here at my favorite place with my beloved godson. "What moment divine . . . what rapture serene," I was humming to myself, "and we suddenly know what heaven we're in," remembering Cole Porter's exquisite love song.

Gaby seemed to be totally at ease too. Although I was just about three feet away from him, Gaby suddenly called to me, "Come here, come here," with extreme urgency. As I sat next to him, he added, "Look, look," pointing to the moon. "Can you see this dark spot on the left?"

"Yes, I do, I see spots on the moon, what about it?" I asked, squinting.

"And don't you see the two eyes and the nose and the mustache?" Gaby kept asking.

"Well, let me see . . . yes, I see something like two eyes," I replied, looking.

"And the nose and the mustache?" Gaby insisted, getting excited.

"You mean it's like someone's face?" I mused.

Gaby totally surprised me when he declared with absolute authority, "It's Baba, it's Baba's face, he is watching us." Of course I agreed with him. Nothing could make me happier than witnessing Gaby's open spirit. The rays of the moon on the water seemed to be licking our feet. It was as if Baba's moon face was extending its rays all the way down and reaching out to us, touching our eyes and hearts with infinite sweetness.

Over the years, Gaby had seen many photos of Meher Baba, in my home, in some of my friends' homes, and right here in his bedroom, so he knew the strong, unmistakable features of Meher Baba's face, but that Gaby would allow himself to express this kind of mystical experience was miraculous!

He certainly would not have shared this in his regular environment, where he was too scared of being ridiculed by "the boys." With me he was safe. He knew that I loved "that kind of stuff," as he often put it, but that's not why he just got it. I was certain that this was a spontaneous and totally genuine experience for him, and I was glad to see that the right-brain Gaby was still alive and showing him another dimension.

I also knew how much Gaby longed to be seen. Meher Baba, with his full moon face, was seeing him, looking at him, watching over him, for real, as a matter of fact. I felt very proud of him, my godson, who could feel connections between the visible and invisible worlds. I was also overjoyed that my mystical devotion had rubbed off on him and that I could be of service on this level as well.

A few days later, we went to the Meeting Place of the Center for an evening of music performance. Gaby and the pack of teenagers had been told to show up for the concert, and they did.

On the walls were exhibited Will David's new, beautiful paintings, all showing outdoor landscapes, different views and moments at the Center.

"Look," said Gaby, "look, here it is, look at this," pulling me by the sleeve to one of the paintings.

"Wow," I acquiesced, startled. "Yes, here it is. Wow!"

It was a small oil painting showing exactly what we had witnessed on the full moon night at the lake, with the deck, the rays of the moon on the rippling waters, and Baba's face in the full moon. Someone else had the same experience! Gaby was very excited and proud to see his sixth sense being affirmed.

A few days later, I managed to buy the painting from Will. It's now hanging in my home, and when I see it with soft eyes, I hum again, "What moments divine . . . what rapture serene . . . and we suddenly know what heaven we're in."

When Gaby looks at the picture nowadays, he mutters, "That was really freaky!" But he stares at it every time he comes to my home.

Chapter 22

Music Medicine

"Music fills the infinite between two souls."
—*Rabindranath Tagore*

It was with my singing voice that I had bonded with Gaby the first time I saw him as a newborn, in the intensive care unit. All the clicking noises of computers keeping track of the six newborn babies in the room faded away. It was just Gaby and me in our sweet bubble. For the next ten days, I returned to his side, tuned in to his heartbeat, and chanted very softly to his ear a favorite mantra, *Om namah Shivaya,* which means: I bow to the Spirit fully alive in you. His eyes were closed. He did not see me, but I knew he heard my healing sounds.

I had discovered the healing power of chanting at the Indian ashram. After returning to ordinary life, chanting kept coming to me spontaneously all the time, showering, driving, walking, sitting, dancing, and it remained my way of connecting to my inner self, to my feelings and emotions, whether grief or joy, to my desires and dreams, and to the deep love in my soul.

During the years I cared for Gaby as a baby, whenever he was crying, I chanted the same mantra to him, always softly, sharing with him, again and again, the same love and presence I had felt for him the first time. He would look at me for an instant, then close his eyes and become totally peaceful as he recognized the chant and was comforted by it. The story goes that Gaby started singing before he was talking. He actually got into talking around three years old, which is considered late, but when anyone worried about it and asked whether his stroke could be the cause of this delay, someone would offer: "Do you know Einstein did not talk before he was three?"

But Gaby was not silent. He was discovering all the sounds he could make. He had heard a lot of music while still in the womb, mostly violin played by his father practicing, and once out of the womb, he seemed more interested in listening to himself creating his own sounds than getting into speaking words.

Our singing bond expanded when six-year-old Gaby started going to the Berkeley Ecole Bilingue, a French-American school. When I picked him up after school, he would skip out singing the French children's songs I had learned as a kid, like:

Coucou, hibou, coucou
dans la forêt lointaine, on entend le hibou,
du haut de son grand chêne, il répète coucou,
coucou, hibou, coucou hibou
coucou hibou, coucou!

(Cuckoo, owl, cuckoo
In the distant forest, we can hear the owl,
From the top of the big oak, it repeats

Cuckoo, owl, cuckoo owl,
Cuckoo owl, cuckoo!)

This song became our new mantra, the two of us sharing the fun of repeating the words in different tunes, call-and-response style, as we drove from school to my home to his home, to friends' homes, and back.

The Beatles were Gaby's first heroes. I bought all their cassette tapes for the car. Gaby, sitting in front, would select his Beatles tape for the ride and sing along in his crystalline boy voice. It was easy for Gaby to learn new songs, melodies, and harmonies. He already had an amazing capacity for memorizing the lyrics. The words meant a lot to him. He sang them as if they were his own words. Some of them sounded poignant in his voice, like the song entitled "Help". Gaby with his ankle pain and his limp, Gaby who was not yet too self-assured, Gaby who was a little different, could express his vulnerability and his need for support as he sang along. The Beatles made the word "help" an okay word. It was fine to need help, to ask for help, if the Beatles said so. Gaby became one of them.

And of course I loved hearing the call for help and being one of the helping friends.

I also noticed that Gaby loved to sing the Beatles' songs about love, like the famous ones, "All You Need is Love" and "Love Me, Do", lines he would repeat over and over again, feeling safe asking for love, since the Beatles kept begging for it. These words, so fresh and cheerful, were a perfect language for a sensitive kid.

When Gaby was going through the rehab exercises for his right hand, I would sing to him the Beatles song "I Want to Hold Your Hand." Gaby already had beautiful long-fingered hands, but the right one had lost some of the finest movements. I called his right hand "my favorite hand." I would hold it to empower it, one more opportunity for both of us to feel connected.

Gaby was selecting his own mantras. I saw how refrains that carried such simple and pure messages were our Western mantras and how beneficial it felt to keep repeating them.

Soon Gaby started singing with Ellie, his paternal grandmother, who had made a career at the music department of California State University in Hayward, teaching voice and piano, and directing the choir. Ellie was thrilled to have a grandson so gifted musically.

That's when I became interested in the musical genes of the family. Where did they come from? Did Ellie come from a musical family? How about Ellie's husband, Simon, who died the year before Gaby was born? What was his connection to music?

Those questions took me on a long journey back to the Ukraine before the Russian Revolution. That's when Ellie's parents came to the United States. Her mother, Ginda, arrived at Ellis Island in 1911 by herself at fifteen, after having lost both parents and having barely survived an anti-Semitic Cossack raid of their Ukrainian village. A well-to-do surviving aunt paid for Ginda's trip to New York, where she joined another aunt who lived in a tenement on the Lower East Side.

Ellie's father, Zacharia, also came from the Ukraine. He had gone to a Jewish trade school and had become a good tool and die maker. At the time, the tsar was rounding up all the young men he could find, especially the Jewish ones, to join his army for twenty-five years. The boy could have been abducted and had to escape. At seventeen, he stowed away on a ship going to New York. Getting close to Manhattan, he jumped off the ship since he had no papers, and swam ashore with nothing, having memorized his cousin's address. He arrived safely at the same tenement building where Ginda lived with her aunt. Thanks to his training, Zacharia always had a good job and, five years later, he and Ginda were married.

Nine years later, in 1926, Ellie was born. By then the family lived in New Jersey, had a small candy store open long hours, and lived behind the store, a hand-to-mouth living. That's where Ellie grew up and started showing an interest in music.

Ellie was friends with the girl next door, whose family was better off. They had a piano which Ellie started playing, which led to piano lessons, which led to a scholarship to Montclair State College, where Ellie did two music majors, in piano and choir, which led her to the Manhattan School of Music in New York, where she was accepted into the conductor Robert Shaw's outstanding Collegiate Chorale. By now Ellie could play the piano as an accompanist in exchange for voice lessons. When she sang for Passover at a New York temple she met her future husband, Simon Cohen.

After four years in the US Army in World War II France, and thanks to the GI Bill, Simon had gone to the Manhattan

School of Music, where he majored in voice and got his BA and MA, and where he met Ellie. During the summer, Ellie and Simon were both soloists with the Tanglewood Chorale, and at the end of the season, they were married. It was music that brought them together.

The new couple eventually moved to Oakland, California, where Simon got his second job as cantor at Temple Beth Abraham.

Settled in Oakland, Ellie became fully involved with her true passion, music. She was the conductor of a choir for adults in Berkeley. She was a professional soloist in the Oakland Symphony Orchestra and gave piano and voice lessons at home. She went back to school at California State University in Hayward. When she completed her MA magna cum laude, Ellie, a born teacher, was instantly hired by the music department and thrived there until her retirement.

The couple had three sons. Ellie said, "I made sure they would all learn a stringed instrument so that we could form a quartet with me as the pianist." Ellie planned her whole life around music.

Jeremy, Gaby's father, is now a virtuoso violinist, who plays both classical and jazz music. He is a composer, arranger, and the head of his own successful group, Quartet San Francisco.

Joel, Gaby's uncle, and his ex-wife are professional cellists. Josh, the other uncle, is now the conductor of the Castro Valley Orchestra and is married to an accomplished flutist.

Of his generation, Gaby is the only one who has stuck to music.

Gaby singing and Ellie at the piano

I drove Gaby to his voice lessons with grandmother Ellie, always stayed in the room with them, and enjoyed listening. Gaby was learning songs from popular musicals like *West Side Story,* and even as an eight-year-old child, he could sing a romantic song with passion. He easily learned the fast, intricate words of "My Favorite Things" from *The Sound of Music,* and could sing it by heart in the car as we drove back home.

One day, Ellie turned to me. "How about you? How come you are not singing?" she asked in her usual blunt way, as if it was a sin not to sing.

"I am very happy just listening," I answered, "although I have done a lot of chanting in the past."

"Come here, stand by the piano, and repeat!" Ellie ordered.

We got through the warm-up. I heard my voice coming out, felt myself getting excited, and Ellie exclaimed, "You have a beautiful soprano voice! You've got to use it!" And that's how I started taking voice lessons with Ellie and soon joined a choir.

Singing for me was, like chanting had been, a way to open my lungs, my breathing, my chest, my throat, and my heart. It gave me a tremendous feeling of well-being, aliveness, and love for all. Gaby and I were sharing the same practice of opening ourselves, with the help of the same voice coach.

For his ninth birthday, Gaby was now big enough to receive as a present a French horn, the French horn being the only instrument played by the left hand, while the right hand is just cupped in the bell of the horn. That was perfect for Gaby, whose right fingers had not totally recovered all the finest skills.

I had never held a horn like this one—saxophones or trumpets, yes, but not a French horn with its amazing twenty feet of tubing.

"Are you really strong enough to blow air into a twenty-foot-long tube and have a sound come out?" I asked, bewildered.

"I am strong, and I will get stronger, I am a big guy, I'll show you," replied Gaby proudly, pressing his shining brass horn to his chest as if it was already part of him. And he did show me, and all of us, that he had the power of sounding his horn. When he was practicing, I used to sing to him the lyrics from Cole Porter's high-energy song "Blow, Gabriel, Blow!"

Gaby with his new French horn

Gaby joined a series of brass bands: the Albany Middle School Symphonic Band, the Diablo Wind Symphony, the Cazadero Performing Arts Concerts. It never crossed my mind that I could miss any of the concerts, except of course when they went on tour to Scandinavian countries.

When Gaby's voice changed at eighteen, it was time for him to go to college. He applied to study voice and theater at the California Institute of the Arts in Valencia, Los Angeles County, and was accepted. He loved his voice teacher, sang all year, and when he came back home, he declared, very self-assuredly, that he had given up the horn and that his voice was now his instrument.

After a year away, Gaby decided he would rather live in the East Bay, close to family and friends, and enrolled in the music department at the California State University East Bay in Hayward, where Ellie, now retired, had taught for twenty-seven years. That's where Gaby met his inspiring new teacher, Professor Buddy James, director of choral and vocal studies, and choir conductor of both the classical choir, East Bay Singers, and the jazz choir. Gaby joined both.

Buddy James always took his choir members on a weekend retreat at the beginning of the new college year. The students took the bus together and spent their time singing, eating, sleeping, playing, walking in the woods, and basically getting to know and bond with one another. When Nicole and I met Buddy James a week later, at the first performance of the choir, he told us, "Something new happened at the retreat. The students enjoyed meeting each other, flowed easily through the schedule, no one was left out, no one complained, they all had fun and became a solid group. I was happily surprised, and I realized that it was Gaby's joie de vivre and easygoing ways that had created the mood. He was the social glue."

Gaby loved everything about choir singing and choir performing. Harmonizing with others fulfilled his need for belonging and happiness. It was perfect medicine for him.

Their repertoire included a wide variety of music. I asked Gaby, "What is your favorite music? What do you want to get into? Jazz? Pop? Musicals? Opera?"

"I don't know yet, I have to see what I am good at, probably R&B, soul, jazz," he mused.

"How about hip-hop?" I asked.

"I got into it when my brother bought his first hip-hop CD and kept buying a whole collection of them," explained Gaby. "It was really his thing."

"Yes," I reminded him, "you had a phase when you were singing 'The Valley of the Shadows.' You knew the whole long song by heart, and you were really good at remembering the words and the beats."

"I still like hip hop, yeah, like Coolio, Tha Dogg Pound, Snoop Dogg, Wu-Tang. And Tupac, of course, and Kanye West, and Peter Gunz, and Notorious."

There was also Bob Marley in Gaby's life. When he moved into his new apartment in Hayward next to Cal State, the first thing that went on the wall was a full life-size poster of Bob Marley standing next to his guitar. And Gaby's solo of Bob Marley's "No Woman, No Cry" for the choir was his first big solo success. He loved Bob Marley's wild sense of freedom and felt part of his tribe.

When I went to visit Gaby at his home, he played for me on YouTube the music he was exploring that week. He listened to all kinds of fabulous songs and singers, sang along with them, and kept checking voices and styles to see what resonated with his range and his soul.

For the weekly movement-to-music class that I have been leading for years, I often play the songs and musicians that I discovered or rediscovered with Gaby. One week I'll play the songs of Elton John, the next week the songs of

Donny Hathaway, Dean Martin, Ray Charles, Stevie Wonder, Michael Bublé, French jazz pianist Michel Petrucciani, Bill Withers, or others—my selections following Gaby's explorations.

Music had come into my life when I went to boarding school at nine, and joined the Gregorian chants choir. We learned and rehearsed all week the chants meant for the next Sunday mass celebration, a big repertoire since every Sunday was different. I loved these choir sessions in the chapel. They were soothing, elevating, and beautiful, they gave me a sense of elation I had never experienced, and they were the perfect music medicine that we all needed after the traumatic years of war.

After boarding school, my singing voice went underground and I just became a listener, although an ardent one, until all that changed when I gave up trying to be an intellectual and arrived in Bombay, India, where I went to my first Indian classical music concert. The sounds of the sitar and the powerful rhythms of the tablas kept touching new parts of me, awakening new emotions. My analyzing mind got turned off, and it was with my whole body that I was listening. I was shaken to my roots. It was spontaneous music therapy, with no therapist other than the music.

When I arrived at the ashram, the chanting sessions, always accompanied with tablas, harmonium and cymbals, pierced my heart, releasing pain and grief one moment, peace or ecstasy the next moment, waves after waves, reawakening the long-lost singer I had been. Chanting became an essential and healing meditation practice.

This was my background when I settled in Berkeley and Gaby was born. My love of music kept growing as Gaby was growing into his own musical journey.

Eventually, it became clear to everybody in the music department that Gaby had not only a good ear, a good pitch, a good sense of rhythm, melody and harmony, plus talent and passion, but also a powerful tenor voice.

I kept urging him, "Gaby, you are so fortunate to have a good voice, nothing makes one happier than singing, it's good for your soul, go for it, keep practicing, give yourself entirely to it, the rest will follow, doors will open," I would repeat, empowered by Joseph Campbell's catchphrase:

"Follow your bliss. . . . If you do follow your bliss, you put yourself on a kind of track that has been there all the while waiting for you, and the life you ought to be living is the one you are living. When you can see that, you begin to meet people who are in the field of your bliss and they open the doors to you."

I felt free to keep advocating. By now I had found my own sources of bliss. I had discovered the healing powers of chanting, and the ecstasy of moving to music. I had followed my passion for healing through the awakening of the Shakti, and eventually I had reunited with Dr. Rosen when I found my calling with Rosen Method Bodywork therapy and movement therapy. Gaby was fortunate, having found his calling and his bliss as a child.

Chapter 23

Discovering a New Opera Tenor

"People think I'm disciplined. It is not discipline.
It is devotion. There is a great difference."
—*Luciano Pavarotti*

Gaby was now twenty-three, a voice major at the California State University East Bay in Hayward. At the end of his junior year, he was due to perform his very first formal recital, a rite of passage, before moving into his senior year. It was a big deal.

When Gaby found out the date of his recital, he called me. "Guess what?"

"Tell me," I replied.

"I just got the date for my recital, May seventh, on your birthday," he told me with a trace of anxiety. "Will it be OK for you? Will you be able to come?"

"Of course I will come," I replied with great enthusiasm. "It will be the best birthday gift."

The recital was the focus of Gaby's attention for the next seven months. He had to prepare and present six classical songs. Today kids, born with the Internet, have access from home, at the click of a button, to every voice on the planet and can even see the singers perform on YouTube.

In the old days, all you had were LP records, and if you

wanted to see a performer on stage, you had to wait until he would grace your city's concert hall.

Once he had learned the melody of a song, Gaby would go on YouTube and listen to as many recordings of the same piece sung by different tenors as he could find online. He would select the rendition that inspired him the most, or even parts of different renditions, and then he would play them over and over again, practicing singing along, and emulating the singers.

Then he would record his own rendition and listen to himself. He could hear the spots where he had trouble, and explained in typical youth jargon, "This way I can work shit out of my voice."

He also had his private lessons with his vocal coach, Pam, which he recorded. He would keep practicing the exercises she gave him, which meant making all kinds of sounds. For this he went to a practice room, a cell with a piano, in the music building. He did not want his neighbors to hear him. "Those sounds are too weird and private," he told me.

A few days later, Gaby was visiting me at my home. It was late afternoon and, as we opened my front door to go out, we heard loud female orgasm sounds coming from the cottage next door. Gaby froze in place, shocked and embarrassed, and, looking at me, whispered, "How can she do that?"

"You mean making sounds that are too weird and private?" I asked. "Isn't that what you make in your practice room?"

"But I don't force everybody to hear me," Gaby snapped back.

"And with Pam, you feel OK making all kinds of noises?" I asked.

"Of course, she is my voice teacher," replied Gaby, implying this was a stupid question. It was the job of a voice teacher to make her student explore and liberate his whole body. It created a very intimate relationship between them. Gaby had been feeling totally safe with Pam.

But the practice rooms were OK for exercises only. "These cells are dead, there is no reverb. They kill my songs," Gaby explained. So when it came time to rehearse, he practiced at home, and that's how I heard his songs, over and over again. I became his sounding board, a new delightful assignment, on a continuum with the original one of "You are the blessing," and the second one "Enjoy him," which I kept remembering at every turn of Gaby's life.

Gaby would also take me online and have me listen to the different voices of his favorite tenors. He continued to be very serious about educating me, passing on in his own words what he was learning from his teachers, a delightful part of our relationship since he was little.

That's how I discovered the voice of Fritz Wunderlich, soaring effortlessly. I got to feel, in my own body, how such a pure, easy voice could reach deep inside, how it touched my cells and made them dance with joy. He was a lyric tenor. Pavarotti was another lyric tenor. That was the kind of voice that Gaby, also a lyric tenor, was training to become.

"That's who I want to sound like," Gaby told me, with his usual determination, aware that he had to work on expanding his range.

Finally May 7 arrived. The small campus theater was almost full with Gaby's family, friends, and music students. I arrived early, wearing my favorite silver jacket in honor of my birthday and in honor of my godson, and sat next to grandmother Ellie. We read the program together. She knew all the songs and was impressed with the selection. I was feeling nervous and excited, sitting at the edge of my seat, filled with expectation.

Gaby's songs had to be in three different languages, so he had selected two in French, two in German, and two in English.

Gaby walked on stage with a piano major, Tristram, his buddy and accompanist, both formally dressed, not in tuxedos but in their best suits. Gaby wore a brown suit, a black shirt with a brown-and-blue tie, and his dressy black shoes. His face was glowing, and he was obviously very excited to be on stage. Tristram was all in black. From where I was sitting, I realized that they were not teenagers anymore. They had grown into men, real and handsome men.

They bowed to the audience, settled in, checked in with one another, ready and go.

After Tristram played a few measures, Gaby's voice cried out Handel's famous lyrics, "Comfort ye, my people," strong but not pushy, full but not overwhelming, in a clean pitch but not dry, brilliant and effortless, a powerful moment. I took a deep breath. I felt my whole body drop into my seat and my brain relax. This was the moment I had dreamed of witnessing for years, and it was perfect.

God, speaking through Gaby's voice, was saying: Comfort ye, my people, do not worry, I am aware of your pain. It will be over soon, you have suffered enough, you have redeemed yourself, and you are forgiven. It was as if Gaby was channeling God.

"Comfort ye," the leitmotif, was repeated three more times, the melody stretching it, amplifying it, as if wanting to reach all ears and hearts everywhere. I heard authority and compassion in Gaby's voice. Gaby, who is Jewish, understood in his genes the pain of his people, and his genes were chanting in his voice. Gaby had also experienced his own pain and the need to be comforted. It was quite amazing that he chose such a personal song for his first ever to perform publicly.

Then Gaby threw himself into the gorgeous verse: "Ev'ry valley shall be exalted, and ev'ry mountain and hill made low; the crooked straight, and the rough places plain."

This was a song of triumph, and a triumphant beginning for Gaby. He bowed and exited.

I felt uplifted by the spiritual energy. The whole room was filled with the glory of the music and the presence of spirit. The family members looked at one another in awe. Gaby was raised, like the valleys, by the musical text, and the text was raised by Gaby's delivery .

Gaby returned with his accompanist, for a very different mood with a song by Gabriel Fauré.

I was familiar with Fauré, a master of the *mélodie* style, who composed many romantic, exquisite songs in French. One of them, called "Mai," I have sung every year to celebrate the month of May, the month my mother, Gaby, and I were all born. The month of May in Europe is the month most praised and has inspired many songs from all kinds of songwriters.

Gaby performed two songs of Fauré in his excellent French accent. The first one, "Après un rêve," was about a dream of the perfect love, but the lover wakes up and cannot bear the loss of his love. He calls to the night, "Give me back my dream."

> *Reviens, reviens, radieuse,*
> *Reviens, ô nuit mystérieuse.*

Gaby seemed to float in the dreamy atmosphere of the song. It was natural for him; he was not eager to embrace the challenges of material life and preferred to hang out in his imaginary world. Moreover, I had noticed that when Gaby spoke French with me, another part of him showed up, more innocent and intimate. It seemed to be happening when he sang French songs as well.

The next one was a song of despair, from the short opera *Down in the Valley*, by Kurt Weill, a Jewish composer who had to flee Nazi Germany and had lived through despair himself. It was about a desperate, lonely boy, who is about to be hanged, searching in vain with his eyes for his girl, begging for her presence, asking "Where is the one who will mourn me," as if he is sobbing through the song. Gaby's rendition touched my wounded heart. It was a *cri du coeur*.

After the intermission, Gaby was back with the second

song by Fauré, called "En prière," another song of supplication. This time it was Jesus imploring his Father—through Gaby's voice—to grant him the necessary gentleness to ease the suffering of humanity, as he is about to be crucified. Again, I felt how the words evoked what Gaby had experienced growing up. It was true that the hardships he had known had made him gentle, with an open heart to the suffering of others.

Fauré's beautiful, poignant songs were difficult to sing, because they were mostly in *passaggio* mode, the passage between the two registers of the voice, when it was very important to keep the voice "in the mask," as Gaby had explained. He had made me listen to the different sounds created when his voice was vibrating in his face and when it was not. It made a big difference. I could appreciate how well he had just sung.

Then came "Adelaide," another story of love and longing, a haunting melody.

Adelaide is the name of an idealized and unattainable woman, surrounded by a landscape of light, flowers, stars, bells, and a nightingale. The lover's longing is followed by his ecstatic flight into his own death, when he is finally united with his beloved.

This was the ultimate tragic-romantic theme, the lover obsessing about the loved one, calling upon nature to witness his breaking heart. The movement of the song flowed like the ebb and flow of a deep ocean, and suddenly, in a crescendo, it rose like a tsunami and drowned us in its all-embracing passion.

This was also the climax of the recital. And again it

matched something about Gaby, who had already suffered deep disappointments.

Finally the last song, "Die Mainacht," or "A Night in May," by Brahms.

With another nightingale, another search for the beloved, it was a song of loss and sadness, the longing of the soul.

Gaby told me later that this last one was his favorite song, the most beautiful, but by the end of the recital he was exhausted, and he did not serve it as well as he had wished. He was very sad about that. I had not noticed. I was admiring the enchanting melody; I was in an altered state, in awe and wonder at the beauty of the music and its servant.

Gaby received a standing ovation, having made everyone realize what a beautiful, powerful voice he had developed in the last year. He bowed professionally.

After expressing his warm thanks to Pam, who was standing at the back of the theater, Gaby announced to the audience, "Today is my godmother Odile's birthday, and three days ago it was my birthday, so we are going to celebrate out in the lobby. Would you please join us?"

In the lobby we found a reception set up, with two long tables covered with white tablecloths filled with colorful snacks and sodas, plus a birthday cake for Gaby and for me. Listening to our "Happy Birthday" song, the two of us, holding the knife together, cut the first piece of our cake.

Since meeting Gaby as a newborn, this was the happiest day of my new life in Berkeley. The synchronicity of my birthday and Gaby's first recital was magical.

When I reflected on the content of the recital I was

Gaby after performing at the Oakland Cathedral, CA

struck by the spirituality of the evening. Gaby rehearsed many, many hours until the songs—music and lyrics—were fully internalized and became second nature. It was his meditation practice, his path to his true nature. He was fertilizing his soul, focusing on the greatest human feelings of compassion, forgiveness, joy, love of nature, yearning for love and oneness, longing to serve God, and also the deep sadness of separation. He seemed to be open to and familiar with such universal sentiments. He sang God's voice and Jesus' voice. Gaby was devoted to his path. His devotion to his art was palpable. The words became mantras, the music gave depth and power to the words, and his heart kept growing.

Later on, I wanted to share with Gaby about the concept of "rasa" in classical Indian music.

"Rasa," I explained, "is the emotion the musician is striving to convey. It's often translated as 'nectar' because it has the exquisite capacity to touch the innermost soul of the listener."

But Gaby was only concerned with his technique and replied, "I was in my technical bubble, the placement of my voice, watching my *appoggio*. Whatever you felt is your own thing. And I have to work on my diction," he added. "I know it's too slow and it's holding me back, and my breath mechanism has to improve."

"Yes, of course," I concluded, "what I felt was my own thing, and it was nectar to my soul. Out of the nine rasas, I experienced seven of them listening to you: love, beauty, joy, sadness, awe, peace, and courage, and to feel so deeply such rich emotions was truly the best birthday gift."

Chapter 24

My Opera Music Initiation as
a Teenager

When I listened to Gaby practicing the different arias he was working on, we would set it up with me sitting in front of him as the audience, and him standing at the other end of the room as the performer. Both of us played our roles impeccably. Except once. Gaby was singing Rigoletto's famous aria "*La donna e mobile.*" I suddenly found myself singing along, but instead of singing the lyrics in Italian like him, I was singing them in French.

Gaby was startled. "Why do you sing it in French? It's an Italian opera, by Verdi," he reprimanded me.

I was surprised as well. But in a flash it all came back to me. I saw her in her red coat, the way I had seen her the very first time, and instantly remembered her name, Claude Delsalle.

It was the first day of October 1952, *la rentrée,* back to boarding school, a sort of second home for me where I had already spent five years. The so-called *grandes vacances* were over. We were folding ourselves back into our familiar school year, as our summer clothes went back to their closets.

Our Catholic boarding school, called Notre-Dame des Oiseaux, was located one hour by train from Paris, on the outskirts of Verneuil, a sweet village surrounded by small farms, forests, and the meandering river Seine. The locals called our school Le Château; it had belonged to some aristocratic family before it became a convent.

Accompanied by our mothers, a whole group of us returning girls, ages nine to fifteen, met at the Paris Gare Saint Lazare, on the platform of our train, as we had done many times before. We all wore the same navy blue uniform, which included our winter coat and a beret. The beret was navy blue too, and had a flying blue bird stitched on it. We were the birds, *les oiseaux*, flying away from our summer homes like migrators, as the season changed.

One girl was not wearing navy blue. She had on a bright red coat with a tight black belt showing off her curves. Her mother, standing next to her, looked like a movie star, with dyed blond hair, high heels, and lots of fur. I instantly felt drawn to them, but I was too reserved to approach them. Here was a very different animal in our zoo of females. She was probably fifteen like me, I could tell, and at the same time more womanly, the rest of us still girls. I hoped we were in the same junior class.

The new girl was new but not shy. She seemed excited, as if we were going on some wild adventure. She looked around with a huge smile, bright white teeth, and shining eyes, shaking her gorgeous, long, thick auburn mane from side to side. I kept looking at her.

The principal nun who was greeting everyone on the platform was exceptionally friendly to the girl and her mother, as if she had known them years ago when the girl was still a child.

On the train, I sat by a window as I always did. The

new girl did not sit down. She talked to everyone who kept standing like her, laughing all the time. Her name, I overheard, was Claude.

One hour later, we arrived at the small railroad station of our village. All of us spilled out of the train with bags of all sizes that we threw into a horse carriage, and we walked empty-handed for two-thirds of a mile to the convent, most of us chatting and giggling.

I loved the feeling of returning to my country home, with the smells of fallen leaves and the autumn colors, reconnecting with old friends, girls I had lived with day-in, day-out since we were nine years old, and with nuns who had become mothers to us. In fact, we called them *ma mère*. Le Château really was my home; the one where my parents lived in Paris was their home.

So who was this new girl? What was she doing here? Why was her mother so friendly with the nuns? Were they family? What was so special about these two?

I admired Claude quietly for a while. She was gorgeous even after getting into the navy blue uniform, and she often burst into contagious laughter. It took me a few weeks to become friends with her—me the quiet introvert focused on learning, she the bold extrovert wanting to have a good time. But when it happened it changed my life.

Claude loved to talk about herself, and I was already a listener. She was born and raised in Hanoi, then the capital of French Indochina. She went to the boarding school of Les Oiseaux, the same religious order, in Dalat, near Hanoi, a hill station for the French VIPs. The nuns went back and forth between the different schools of the order. Our head nun had known her and her family for many years overseas. The family had recently moved back to France. The colonies were not safe anymore. They had just spent the summer at Royan, a well-to-do beach resort on the Atlantic coast. Claude was fifteen and had been elected beauty queen at the beach beauty contest, and as a result she had been surrounded by lustful boys and men. Her mother, thinking Claude was much too young for all that, had decided to send her back to the convent.

Claude grew up in a world of artists. Her mother was an opera singer and voice coach. The French, believing in their *mission civilisatrice,* made a point of taking their culture with them. In Hanoi, that meant having a grand opera house modeled after the Paris Opera, giving performances similar to the ones in France. Claude had spent her after-school hours in the backstage area of the opera, hearing countless rehearsals of the main famous operas, or at home hearing her mother teaching endless voice lessons. I was fascinated.

There were no artists in my family, only doctors, lawyers, judges, and professors. But I had a musical education. I was a member of the *Jeunesse Musicale.* I had been to the Paris Opera, to the Opéra Comique, and to classical music concerts. I had seen artists on stage and always envied them, but I never had personal contact with any.

At the convent, we had weekly *solfège* (the basics of music) classes. We sang in a choir. So I knew I could carry a tune, that I had a good ear and a good voice.

One Sunday as we were coming out of the chapel after

our morning choir performance, Claude whispered to me, "These chants put me to sleep, I am ready to go back to bed. *C'est trop monotone. Je préfère l'opéra. C'est plus gai.*"

"*Opéra,*" I echoed, "*t'es pas folle, c'est pas de la musique religieuse!*" (Opera, you are crazy, it's not religious music.)

But I got the message: too much Gregorian singing, not enough Opera! *Que faire?* (What to do?)

Claude decided to teach me her repertoire of arias. We did have free afternoons on Sundays, but where could we go? How about in our big park? The central lawn had been transformed into our sports fields, but it was surrounded by *allées,* tall oaks, thick shrubs and bushes, and at the far side, a wall of trees that separated the convent from the rest of the world, creating a refuge where we could get lost or at least have some privacy and not be heard.

We did not need scores. Claude had it all inside her and was eager to show and tell.

She would sing an aria and make me repeat after her until I knew the tune. Then she sang it at the top of her lungs and pushed me until my voice got louder and louder, as loud as hers, and then we would sing it as a duet. It was very exciting. Claude turned into the coach her mother had been.

So far my vocal expressions, whether speaking or singing, were restrained, as was the rest of me. After all, we were learning good manners in order to become the perfect wives of important husbands. But Claude never had to follow that path. On the contrary, in her world, the more emotional, the more expressive, the better. I had been longing to feel this power every time I had seen it on stage. She unleashed in me a voice I did not know I had, my emotional voice. And she also woke up the rebel in me.

The first aria I learned was the famous one from *Madame Butterfly*, about a woman waiting for her beloved. It hit a chord in my wounded heart, and from day one I felt something that I had never felt doing Gregorian chants. Singing at the top of my voice opened up my senses, my emotions, my desires, my will, my whole being.

I kept learning other famous arias from *Carmen*, from the *Marriage of Figaro*, from *Rigoletto*, from *Pagliacci*, and many others Claude remembered, whether sopranos, mezzos, or tenors, male or female roles; and whether the lyrics were in Italian or German, Claude sang them in their French translation, the way she had heard her mother sing them.

Soon we all dispersed for the Easter vacation. When we returned, Claude, boiling with excitement, told me about a new movie she had just seen in Paris with her mother, *The Great Caruso*. It came out of Hollywood in 1951 with Mario Lanza, a fabulous tenor himself, playing the role of Caruso, with a cast of great opera singers singing many of the arias Claude had been teaching me.

"You must see it, it's the best, you must, you must, you must!" she repeated, getting carried away. She took her role as my "initiatrix" very seriously, and of course I wanted to follow her and even become like her.

"But when? Our next vacation is in three months, and what if it's not playing any more in June?" I responded anxiously. (We did not go back home on weekends in those days.)

That's when we started plotting. "I could go next Sunday afternoon," I joked.

"What do you mean?" she asked.

"Well, I could run out after lunch, take a train, go to the movie theater right next to Gare Saint Lazare, run back to the train, and be here in time for dinner. *Ni vu, ni connu*" (nobody will know), I imagined wickedly.

"Ah, ah!" said Claude, impressed, "and how are you going to get out of here without being stopped by the sister *portière?*"

"I don't know," I shrugged. "It was just a fantasy." But Claude got into it.

"I have an idea. Let's check out the other gate, you know the one they unlock for us only when we are walking to the train station, on the other side of the park."

We did, and found out I could slip right through the space between the gate and the wall.

"*Tu vas faire le mur!*" Claude exclaimed with pure joy. (You are going to go through the wall!)

Our plan worked. On Sundays, we were free from after lunch until dinnertime at seven P.M., which gave me ample time for the train rides and the two hours of movie time. Of course, we were supposed to stay within the walls of the estate, but never mind the honor system!

I came back in time, slid back into my conforming self for dinner—*ni vu, ni connu*—but felt on top of the world, empowered by Caruso and by my successful adventure.

I had discovered passion, and we continued our passionate singing in our private corner of the park. Between our sessions, I kept humming the melodies. I felt alive.

When the summer came, we parted to our different worlds, planning to meet again in the fall. But I did not go back. I had outgrown the convent. Claude did not come back either, I was told, and I never saw her again.

She had been a transformative meteor dropped into my life by the gods of opera music. What a preparation for the future godmother of an opera singer!

And yes, in those days, the French translated all the opera lyrics into French. They still believed in their dominance! Not anymore. No one would dare sing an Italian opera in any other language today! In fact, later on, Gaby would have to master the four main opera languages in order to enter the Conservatory of Music.

Chapter 25

BA Senior Recital

Gaby handed me an invitation in the form of a flyer that read:

> The Department of Music presents in Senior Recital,
> Gabriel Liboiron-Cohen, tenor,
> With Dr. Jeffrey Sykes, piano,
> Saturday, May 14, 2011 / 7:30 pm
> Music Building Recital Hall,
> California State University East Bay, Hayward, CA

A year later, Gaby's final recital at California State University East Bay was more formal and demanding. This was his graduation performance for his BA in Music.

I had arrived at Gaby's home early, two hours before the recital, to give him a ride to campus, better than his taking the bus or riding his bike on this momentous day. My whole day was focused on this event, from morning until night. It was his event, and it was also a big event for me, since I had committed myself to supporting Gaby through college in whatever endeavor he chose.

He got into his performing outfit, rented at the local Selix Formalwear store. It was a brown-on-brown pin-striped suit with a silky waistcoat and brown shoes, an orange-and-brown paisley tie, and a pocket hankie, all in the same golden tones as his long, slicked-back hair and well-cropped goatee. The bright white collar of his shirt brought out his large face and his wide, imposing forehead.

After dropping Gaby at the music building, I still had time to kill before the recital. I took a walk around campus, where I had met with Gaby many times, and where Gaby had been thriving. It was a gorgeous location, on the crest of the East Bay hills, with a full view of the Bay, and San Francisco floating in the distance. It might be my last time here, I realized.

I also roamed the corridors of the music building. Checking out announcements on the walls, I discovered Gaby's posters, which he had created on Photoshop to advertise his recital to his peers. They were very funny.

One of them was titled "I WANT YOU," a take on US Army posters, showing Gaby as Uncle Sam, wearing a top hat and long beard, pointing at the reader: "I want you at my senior recital."

The other poster was a picture of Gaby screaming, ready to press a red button saying "KICK ASS," and adding "I'm going to do it . . . Pav it up . . . at my senior recital," meaning Pavarotti of course!

When I got to the concert hall, still early, the previous recital had just ended and the floor was strewn with rose petals. I saw Gaby, in his formal costume, grab a broom from behind the stage and sweep the floor he was going to stand on. Then he set his lectern, not for his arias, which had to be memorized, but for the list of written acknowledgments he was going to read.

The audience started arriving. Of course Gaby's whole

family was coming, even his cousin David, who had flown in from Boston.

Gaby walked on stage with his familiar limp, went to his lectern, and explained that he was going to dedicate each song to a person who had supported him during his four years at Cal State.

His first dedication was to his special voice teacher, Pam. He shared with us how he could go from utter frustration to feeling on top of the world in a one-hour voice lesson, that it was never as hard as he made it, and that he was now sure that all he wanted in life was to learn how to sing.

"Well said!" I told myself, impressed and excited that Gaby would so candidly declare himself.

His first aria, "Il mio tesoro," of Don Ottavio from Mozart's *Don Giovanni*, was a difficult piece, the most demanding of the recital. Gaby flew through it with great tempo and stamina. His right hand was resting on the piano, his head gently swaying to the music, his body well grounded, his gaze fixed high up in front of him, a powerful presence.

Dr. Sykes, the virtuoso pianist; Gaby as Don Ottavio in a fit of revengeful outrage; and Mozart, having fun, no doubt, supervising from on high—the three of them, composer, pianist, and singer, were quite a team of passionate and fun-loving ones, electrifying each other.

At first, I was on edge, rooting for Gaby with all my energies, but soon, once he had mastered the first high notes, my eyes filled with tears of joy, awe, gratitude, pleasure, and ease. Gaby was in charge. "There is nothing to worry about," I told myself, "just enjoy yourself, enjoy him, be the happy witness. It's bliss time!"

I had heard Gaby rehearse this aria many times, at home in his boxer shorts, in the car while driving together, in my living room, in the kitchen, but nothing compared to the fully internalized, embodied result. It was as if I was hearing it for the first time.

Gaby waited for Dr. Sykes to stand and join him. They bowed together to an ecstatic audience and left the stage.

Gaby had to present seven contrasting pieces in four different languages, including two classical arias, three romantic art songs, and two twentieth-century songs.

The second piece, composed by Schumann, was "Dichterliebe," or "A Poet's Love." Gaby explained that he was introduced to these songs when listening to Fritz Wunderlich online, that he fell in love with Fritz's voice and that he wanted to sing like him, or at least sing the songs Fritz sang. Fritz was a tenor who had started on the French horn like Gaby. I had watched Gaby getting more and more enamored of Fritz, Fritz becoming his new idol and role model, "the frizzier of all," he used to joke.

Gaby was singing about love, the poet's love becoming his love. Since he was a baby Gaby had been transparent about his need and longing for affection, always reaching out for contact and tender loving care. Love had been his forte and his realm.

I was deeply touched by how Gaby delivered these romantic songs. He was pouring his heart out, from the ecstasy of shared love to the sadness of loss. And his heart was contagious.

Afterwards, I asked David, Gaby's cousin, who is half Austrian and bilingual, "How was Gaby's German? Did you understand every word?"

"Oh, yes," David answered, "every single word; his German is perfect."

I was not surprised. Gaby has had a gift for languages and can be hilarious imitating different accents, especially doing singsong Indian English! When he was younger, if he wanted to make me laugh, he would launch into it and I would be in stitches! Then he would ask, "How about Irish?" and he would do that, too!

After the intermission, Gaby saved a special moment to acknowledge Dr. James.

Dr. James, the head of vocal studies and the director of choral programs, a jovial, white, corpulent, tall man like Gaby, had been Gaby's strong ally. He had directed several gorgeous choral concerts in which Gaby sang solos. Dr. James took his choir one year to Mexico, and the next to Lithuania, to the greatest delight of his students. Dr. James was also a huge sports fan who had learned from the famous football coach John Wooden.

Coach Wooden, I learned, worked his teams through a process called "The Pyramid of Success." Dr. James adopted the same model to train his students. The twenty-five blocks needed to build the Pyramid of Success represented the twenty-five behaviors necessary to achieve it, from industriousness to enthusiasm, including skill, confidence, friendship, intentness, loyalty, etc. At each chorus rehearsal, the students were asked to focus on one specific block. Today

Gaby told his beloved mentor, "For me, you are an example and a model of each and every one of the twenty-five behaviors."

Dr. James was building not only a great chorus, but also well-rounded young people, as exemplified by Gaby, who had matured impressively in the last four years.

Of the third song, "La Vie Antérieure," a poem by Baudelaire put to music by the French romantic and mystic composer Henri Duparc, Gaby said, "This is a French art song about past lives, and there is no more fitting person to dedicate it to than to my French godmother, Odile. Without you I would be scared shaking in a corner somewhere. Without your constant support and encouragement, I would not be who I am today, and I most certainly would not have done this without you."

I felt my chest swelling with pride and joy. Gaby had often heard me refer to the concept of past lives in our conversations, but he would make a face or would laugh at me, showing me it was all woo-woo new age stuff to him. Today, thanks to this song, I felt that Gaby was honoring my belief system. What a good surprise!

The song evokes a past life lived in a fabulous tropical paradise, and the deep grief of having lost it. The music, the lyrics, and Gaby's voice took us to majestic heights and then dropped us into haunting nostalgia, with passion in every breath.

The next song from the twentieth century, was by British composer Ralph Vaughan Williams, from "Songs of Travel."

Gaby mentioned another of his heroes, Jon Vickers,

the great Canadian tenor, who turned out to be from Sas-katchewan. Gaby, having a little fun, commented, "Who knew anything came from Saskatchewan except cold air!" and added, "My mother just told me last night that my whole family on my father's side was from Saskatchewan, so essentially I am partly from Saskatchewan too."

I noticed how Gaby loved to find personal connec-tions with his role models.

His next song, "Bright is the Ring of Words," was a celebration of artists, and Gaby quoted Jon Vickers, saying: "We have to sing this song at least once a year to know how important we are." He was reminding us that after artists have died, the beauty of their work remains.

Once, when I was listening to Gaby rehearsing this song at home, I lamented, "See, musicians are remembered for their music; for me as a teacher and therapist, there won't be anything to remember me by."

"Yes, there will," countered Gaby. "There will be your book, your story about being a godmother."

I had mentioned to Gaby that I was writing a book, but I had no idea he had taken it so seriously. Another good surprise! I took this beautiful song to heart, grateful that he was singing it with such deep conviction.

For the fifth song, Gaby walked on stage with his father, Jeremy Cohen, a violin virtuoso who was going to accom-pany his son. Gaby dedicated the song to his grandmother, Ellie Cohen, who had been his first voice teacher when he was three years old, and was now sitting in the audience. We got to witness the pride of the musical lineage from grand-mother, to father, to Gaby, son and grandson.

The music had been recently composed, the lyrics from a poem by Emily Dickinson.

Some things that fly there be,
Birds, hours, the bumble-bee:
Of these no elegy.

Some things that stay there be,
Grief, hills, eternity,
Nor this behooveth me.

There are, that resting, rise.
Can I expound the skies?
How still the riddle lies!

I could not follow all the words at first, but was intrigued. When I read the poem later at home, a memory came rushing back again. I saw my seven-year-old self standing in the room where my baby brother was laid to rest. I was facing the window, staring out to the frozen white land, and "expounding the skies," where Nanny said the baby had gone. I was frozen too, as still as the baby in his crib, alone with the mystery of what was happening. "He has gone to heaven, he has become an angel," Nanny had told me. Or in Emily Dickinson's words, "that resting, rise." How could the baby be in his crib and in heaven at the same time? What feels like Eternity is the melancholy of living with the riddle that never goes away. This poem was a blessing. And if the message was about resurrection, here was Gaby, the baby boy who had survived.

Continuing with twentieth-century songs, the sixth

one was dedicated to Zak, Gaby's older brother, who introduced him, when they were children, to the Disney movie *The Sword in the Stone.* This short song, "The Legend of the Sword," was about another of Gaby's heroes, "Arthur the Rescuer." It seemed to me that Gaby had unconsciously identified with the little boy who was a nobody, but had a secret gift and became a king.

The last song was "Pourquoi me réveiller?" (Why wake up?) Gaby dedicated it to "my parents," as if they were still the unit they had not been since they divorced when Gaby was three, twenty-one years earlier. Gaby was still keeping his parents together: "I would not be here without you *two*, obviously. I love you *both*, I dedicate this aria to *both* of you."

This was the swan song of Werther, the young poet who was dying of unrequited love, filled with pathos, screaming out his pain with his last breath, composed by the prolific French opera composer Massenet. Gaby did not hold back. He gave it every ounce of energy he still had. It came out with a grandeur that enlarged my whole being.

Yes, this was the end, a little death for Gaby as well, the end of his time at California State University East Bay, with his beloved teachers and friends. Was that why his recital ended on such a mournful note?

After a standing ovation, Gaby invited us to a reception in the hall where he kept repeating, "Thank you, thank you, you make me happy," with a huge smile.

Around the buffet table full of luscious treats, I caught Dr. Sykes, who walked like a dancer and exuded playfulness.

poster created by Gaby

I asked him, "What makes you think Gaby can become a professional opera singer?"

"Well," he replied, "I have seen many students. I can tell you what I have learned. Some people have a voice. Some people have something to say. And some people have both. They have a voice and they have something to say. Gaby is one of them, he has both. He has the voice needed, and he has something to say. You either have it or you don't. It's not something you can create. He has it. Now he needs to develop it and get it out."

That was Gaby's second standing ovation. I asked myself, "How does he touch people? He is not trying to win the audience, like Maria Callas did." Callas used to say "the audience is your enemy," and that she was going to force them into loving her. Gaby opened his heart. We were deeply touched; we felt with him and for him. Our own hearts opened and we were grateful for his gift to us.

Each song of his recital demonstrated and displayed several qualities that made Gaby who he had become. I recognized the influence of his great teacher and mentor, Dr. James, and the building blocks of his own Pyramid: eagerness and courage, candor, confidence, joy, compassion, and commitment. Greatest of all was his enthusiasm, in the deepest sense of the word: a channel for the gods, a heart filled with spiritual energy.

Chapter 26

MA Final Recital at the San Francisco Conservatory of Music

"The world needs you. Now, the world may not
exactly realize it, but wow, does it need you. It
is yearning, starving, dying for you and your
healing offer of service through your Art."
—Joyce DiDonato

Gaby's application to the San Francisco Conservatory of Music read like a manifesto:

"My goal is to dedicate my life to becoming the best singer I can be," he declared straight away. "I have discovered the joy and passion that come out of me when I fully engage my body, my heart, and my voice. Singing is one of the deepest joys I have experienced. I have learned from my teachers that my voice has the potential to reach an audience. I have the capacity to honestly enter a role and express deep, pure feelings and passion. I have experienced performing for a large audience several times, and I have realized that performing is my forte as well as my greatest joy. Reaching an audience, feeling that I have touched their hearts, is my ultimate goal, and even in the practice room, I am constantly working toward it. I am ready to commit myself to a lifelong journey of practice."

Yes, this was Gaby's manifesto. He was aware of his life's purpose. He understood that he was connecting with something greater than himself. It was his odyssey, his journey toward fulfillment.

Gaby also made a practical appeal, disclosing his special need:

> If I were accepted to different schools, I would
> have to make my decision based on what
> kind of scholarship I am offered. I have been
> living on SSI checks since I was eighteen. The
> California Department of Rehabilitation paid
> my tuition at California State East Bay. I receive
> SSI because of a stroke I had as a newborn,
> which led to a weakened right foot and right
> hand. My disability is not visible. It's just a lack
> of fine motor skills in my right hand and a
> slight limp.

As for his strong points and dreams, he reminded the staff:

> I am fluent in French . . . and I want to become
> a French tenor and sing full lyric roles like
> Des Grieux in *Manon*, and Werther in Jules
> Massenet's operas. As my top develops, I would
> like to take on more challenging roles like Don
> Jose in *Carmen*, by Bizet. I also feel a great love
> for Italian opera; for example, I would like to
> sing Cavaradossi in *Tosca,* by Puccini.

He added:

I always knew I wanted to be a musician, it's
in my DNA. So I took up the French horn as
a child because it is a left-handed instrument,
through which I started my musical training.
When I came into my adult voice I knew I
wanted to undertake the training to be an
opera singer.

Gaby was called back to audition at other universities
where he had applied, but in the end he preferred the San
Francisco Conservatory of Music to stay close to home and
to his support system, emotional and professional. I was
thrilled, of course, that he would be just across the Bay and
that I would still be able to hear his beautiful voice at least
once in a while.

Three times a year there was an "Opera Workshop"
performance at the Conservatory, open to the public, which
I would not miss. These were scenes or snapshots from a specific opera. The students were cast. They learned, rehearsed,
and staged their scenes. They had to inhabit their roles, act
and sing with a partner, not just perform solo arias anymore.

I watched Gaby in the role of Don Ottavio from *Don
Giovanni* by Mozart, a duet in which he was offering love
and comfort to his distressed partner, Donna Anna, who
had just lost her father. I saw how good it was for Gaby
to express his natural compassion. Gaby loved singing to
someone; it was much easier, he said, than singing solos,
and much more satisfying.

Gaby was cast several times in Mozart operas, including in a quintet as Tamino, from *The Magic Flute*, and of course several times in French operas, like *Carmen* by Bizet. At the end of his first year, Gaby had to give his first full recital for examination by a jury. It was not public and I was sorry to miss it, but he was given a written evaluation for each of the five songs he sang (in German, French, Italian, and two in English). Each of the eight voice faculty scribbled their evaluations spontaneously on their jury forms after each song, and handed them to Gaby right after his performance, the evaluations expressing their most immediate and raw reactions to his voice.

Gaby handed me these evaluations. What I read was: "beautiful voice . . . gorgeous instrument . . . great full sound . . . beautiful diction . . . great job . . . very lovely . . . beautiful French," all eight faculty agreeing to great progress, followed by guidelines for improvement.

I was happy to read that several of them wrote "beautiful voice." These were the words I had always used to praise Gaby for his "beautiful voice," thinking it was not a good professional description, but here were the same words from the experts! Beauty touching all of us in its mysterious ways and leaving us at the same loss for more words!

Soon, the second year was upon Gaby before he knew it. It was going to be a very important year because "my final recital will decide my future as an opera singer," he told me. I became part of Gaby's excitement, anxiety, ups and downs of hope, confidence, and doubts. I listened as a rapt audience over and over again to the songs he was preparing to perform.

I was especially struck by the aria of Lenski in *Eugene Onegin* by Tchaikovsky. This was a very long aria in Russian, titled "Kuda, kuda vï udalilis," which means "Where, Where Have You Gone." It's a song of deep regret and sorrow, sung by Lenski before his death.

Gaby had to get a transliteration from the original Cyrillic, study enough Russian words to understand the lyrics, and learn how to pronounce and sing in Russian. He got the help of Sergey, his Russian schoolmate. I heard Gaby practice this aria many times, and I never tired of it. I felt the music and the lyrics touched my melancholic side, which wanted to be touched over and over again.

To graduate, Gaby had to present his recital in front of a jury of four voice faculty who would decide if his examination fulfilled the San Francisco Conservatory of Music standards for the graduate level. It was up to Gaby to choose three songs out of his repertoire. He chose the Lenski aria, "Kuda, kuda vï udalilis," by Tchaikovsky, "Tu Lo Sai" by Torelli, and "Romance" by Debussy.

The next day Gaby was handed the evaluation forms of the four voice faculty filled with glowing words of praise and promise. He learned that he had passed; he was relieved and overjoyed. Gaby was now a Master of Music in Voice Performance, ready to soar through his final Conservatory performance, and share his beautiful voice with total abandon.

The invitation to this final public recital was sent in an email:

San Francisco Conservatory of Music presents:
Gabriel Liboiron-Cohen in Master's Recital,
Carol H. Hume Concert Hall,
Sunday, May 11, 2014, at 8 P.M.

I was sitting in the concert hall early on. I kept social-
izing to a minimum, preparing to be totally present with
myself and with Gaby's performance.

Since the recital date fell on Mother's Day, Gaby started
with his dedication: "To me, Mother's Day has always meant
honoring all the women who have supported me. So I dedicate my entire performance to all the mothers in the house,
and all the mothers who make the world go around and give
an infinite amount of love and support. You are all the rea-
sons we have love in our lives and songs in our hearts."

In this elegant, small, and intimate hall, I became
aware, more than ever before, of the powerful give-and-
take between audience and performer. Here was Gaby,
up on stage, standing in front of us by himself, next to his
piano accompanist, and here we were, about two hundred
of us, seated out in the theater, staring at him, giving him
our full, eager attention. I saw his strong and tall body, his
broad, open chest, his wide forehead, his shining eyes, all of
him facing us, being directly impacted by our high, expect-
ant energy, empowered by it, and transforming it into the
passion and beauty of his vocal performance, which in turn
touched our hearts and souls. What amazing alchemy!

I was no longer just a listener sitting back. I was par-
ticipating with all my energies in Gaby's performance. I

understood anew why Gaby loved to perform, as he had declared so many times. His natural open heart received his audience, took it in, filling his every cell, and his whole being seemed to be singing in his voice. He seemed to become bigger, larger, lighter, freer, more alive, more present, and kept expanding. I was expanding with him. We were all expanding, vibrating together, and becoming bigger than our isolated selves. We were all in communion, opening up to our true nature of love and joy.

Gaby sang eight art songs in French, by Fauré, Debussy, and Lalo. I loved and resonated with the beauty of the melodies, the poetical images and metaphors, and the romantic sentiments that Gaby could express with tenderness and conviction, and sounded so true and fresh in his young man's voice.

For the aria of Prince Tamino, falling in love with Pamina, in Mozart's *Magic Flute*, Gaby had the perfect voice to convey the wonder of love at first sight. The pure tone quality of his voice matched the purity of young Tamino's new love.

Then Gaby sang the Lenski aria from *Eugene Onegin*. He had totally internalized Lenski's feelings of loss and despair. His voice became deeper and deeper, begging his beloved to remember him, as death was approaching. At the end, although I had heard it many times before, I felt stunned, heartbroken. I could hardly get up for the intermission.

After the break, Gaby sang two Italian songs, not love songs any more, but songs of betrayal and disillusion. Gaby could unleash the full power of his voice, almost screaming the rage of the deceived lover.

Gaby dedicated each song to someone in the audience who had supported him, as he had done at his senior recital. His dedication to me of his song "Nell" was so moving I felt my heart melt, almost achingly. I had to clasp my hands on my chest, bend my head and bow.

I was blown away that Gaby could voice his feelings with such conviction. Over the years, like most parents and adults around children and teenagers, I had felt taken for granted at times, and that was fine. I had dedicated myself to the path of selfless service, seva. Seva was my spiritual practice. Gaby had given me plenty of opportunity to serve. I had discovered that service was the source of abiding joy. Gaby was under no obligation to me, I was the one who was obligated to him.

The simple fact that his family allowed me to take on the role of godmother had been a gift; that his mother had included me at newborn Gaby's bedside and that I had been part of Gaby's healing had been a great gift; that Gaby had taught me playfulness and joy had been endless gifts; that I was able to contribute later to Gaby's development as a great singer had been and still was a boon.

But that Gaby, at this turning point of his life, on this momentous day, in public, facing his audience, was able to evoke the gifts he had received from me, felt like the fulfillment of our relationship, a sacred relationship. Of course it was part of the academic tradition to acknowledge your supporters, but Gaby spoke with such sincerity I felt his gratitude was true and deep. We were both grateful, both a blessing to one another. Gaby was becoming an authentic spiritual being. Godmother-godson, we had been a good team.

Godmother-godson after the performance

These are Gaby's words: "For those of you who don't know, I have a godmother, Odile. Since before I was born, she has been a gigantic influence in my life. Anything I ever desired, whether it was kung fu lessons, or horseback riding, or emotional therapy, or shoes, or a ride to an appointment, or help doing my homework, she was there, ready. I can't explain all the fun things we've done, and where I would be without her influence. I wouldn't have learned to meditate or breathe or how to take my time to notice the beauty of simplicity, or how to reframe defeat into life-changing experiences. Someone we regularly referred to as my second mom, Odile, your undying generosity, and the pure love that radiates from you, will never be forgotten. I love you, and so I dedicate 'Nell' in your honor."

"Nell" was a poem written by the famous French romantic Leconte de Lisle and a musical masterpiece composed by Fauré. The poet compared the lover's heart to a red rose in full bloom, which will never fade. Everything else will, but love will never pass: that was the message I heard and received.

Gaby's last song was the famous "Dein Ist Mein Ganzes Herz" (Yours is My Heart Alone) by Franz Lehar, the ultimate romantic melody and passionate lyrics. It was a grand conclusion.

Gaby got his third standing ovation. The charisma I had seen in him as a child I now saw shining through in him as a performer. His teachers, his colleagues, his family and friends stood up to celebrate this great moment of launching a new, up-and-coming young tenor into the world. There was a short reception in the lobby where I watched Gaby—ecstatic—receive innumerable hugs in his wide-open arms. Time to celebrate!

Chapter 27

Looking Back, March 2014

"Attention is the rarest and purest form of generosity."
—Simone Weil

The other day, walking out of my home down Rose Street and turning right on Walnut Street to reach Peet's Coffee, I bumped into Carol just outside the Jewish Community Center (JCC), where Gaby went to preschool. She had been his teacher for two years, before he moved on to kindergarten.

Although it had been more than twenty years since we had met, Carol and I recognized each other.

"Oh, hello, I remember you, you used to come to my classroom," Carol said, looking at me. "Oh yes," she added, "now it's coming back to me, you were Gaby's friend. Gaby," she repeated. "I'll never forget how he came into my life."

I nodded with excitement. Someone else had been touched by Gaby. "Yes," I replied, "I am still Gaby's friend. In fact I am his godmother. I used to pick him up two or three times a week right after your class. Well, now Gaby is twenty-seven years old and he is still a sweet person."

"Well, of course," Carol confirmed, "he was always sweet and will always be sweet. His heart is sweet," she explained.

I was amazed at Carol's awareness; I could see her face lighting up as she was remembering him after so many years.

"Do you remember how he got accepted at the JCC?"
I asked Carol.

This was a typical "Gaby story" that had been told many times by family and friends over the years. When Gaby was ready for preschool, his parents decided that he should go to the Berkeley JCC, but they had not planned ahead. School had already started, and Gaby was not enrolled. He was on the waiting list, way down. So Mom, Dad, and Gaby went to the JCC administration office to plead. While the adults were discussing the admission problems, Gaby slipped away, wandered around the hallway, and came to a classroom where the door was wide open. He saw a group of little children sitting on the floor in a circle listening to their teacher telling them a story.

Carol remembered. "Yes, of course I remember, that's my favorite story. I saw him appear at the door of my class-room. He looked in and stood at the threshold for a while. Then very quietly he walked in the room. He saw a space on the floor between two kids and sat down cross-legged with-out the slightest hesitation, as if this spot had been reserved for him. I was busy telling a story. The children were star-ing at me riveted. When I finished it, I turned to Gaby and asked him, 'Hello, who are you?' 'Gaby,' he replied, with a sense of self that impressed me."

"After class was over, I went with him to the office and explained how Gaby had just showed up, and I added: 'Well, it looks like Gaby belongs in my class. He saw children like himself sitting on the floor, and he sat down.' And that was it," Carol continued. "The director just had to accept him right there and then. Gaby had taken care of himself." And

Carol added, "He was neither shy nor demanding, just trusting himself. I felt connected to him the moment I saw him claim his place in the circle."

Yes, I had heard this story at the time, and now I was happy to hear it again and to know that Carol had cherished the memory of Gaby's appearance.

That classroom had lots of large windows and was full of sunshine. I always came to pick up Gaby a few minutes early so I could watch the end of the class. I would stand by the open door just like he had. I would see him sitting in the circle on the floor next to the teacher, listening intently to the story. A second later, Gaby's head would turn toward the door as if drawn by my presence. I would see a big smile of satisfaction on his face for an instant, and then he would turn right back to the teacher and stay focused until the end of the story. I knew we were deeply connected.

The second year Gaby was at the JCC, when I came to pick him up, the children would be in the courtyard. As soon as Gaby saw me, he ran all over the yard and made me chase him. The other children would get into the chase and protect him from being caught. I was delighted to play their chasing game and made sure to keep it going plenty of time.

It felt like I was being pulled out of myself, invited out into this world of fired-up kids, challenged to share their high energy and run with it like they all did. It was the feeling of pure joy, a joy that needed to be awakened and reawakened over and over again, one of Gaby's lasting gifts.

Then we would walk two blocks to the Juice Bar Collective, a tiny health-food deli takeout with just one small blue table in a corner. "It's my table," Gaby would say, grabbing it before anyone else could.

"Gaby, what do you want today?" I asked.

"Carrot juice and hard-boiled egg," was his consistent response. While I stood in line waiting for my turn to order, I would look around and watch people look at him. He was shining with his thick blond hair, his wide green eyes, his sense of being happy with himself and happy to be seen. I saw people light up when they saw him, and I understood the moment of simple joy they experienced. Gaby was not seeking attention, he was just receiving their smiles, and he did not seem obliged to smile back. He received people with some kind of open presence that was inviting and giving at the same time. I told myself, "Gaby is charismatic, I wonder where that will take him."

I loved sitting at cafes where the same quiet mutual attraction between Gaby and other customers often happened.

Earlier, when Gaby was still in a stroller and I lived on Oregon Street, I would take him to Nabolom, a bakery, kind of a Berkeley institution like the Juice Bar, a few blocks from my home. Gaby would always order the same thing: "Two Tibetan breadsticks, please."

I would have one of my many daily teas. We would sit on the bench outside the bakery and enjoy the street scene. That was something I wanted to share with Gaby, the traditional French pastime of sitting at an outdoor café, sipping something and watching people. I liked the feeling of having eye contact with others without having to talk or engage. Gaby and I were as happy to be seen as we were to be watching, that simple give and take going on in silence.

Epilogue

A Small Miracle, May 2015

*"Miracles are not contrary to nature but only
contrary to what we know about nature."*
—Saint Augustine

I had spent the last two weeks preparing my first full draft
of this story for submission to my coach, trying to make
it look as professional a manuscript as possible. When I
handed off a clean copy, I felt relieved. I had done it, it was
now out of my hands for a while and on its own journey. I
could start preparing for my trip to France.

The first thing to do was to check how much money
I had left in the bank account I had kept in Paris. I went
online as I had done many times before, but I could not
access my bank statements. Frustrated, I called the branch
manager in Paris, and luckily, I did reach him in person. I
explained that I was calling from California, that I would
be in Paris soon and was planning to come and talk to him,
but in the meantime I needed to look at my account. "Why
can't I access my account online as I have always done?
What's going on?" I asked.

"Things have changed recently," he explained. "There
has been so much fraud, you need a new access code to
open your account."

"And how do I get one?" I asked.

"If you give me a moment, I will give you your new access code," he continued.

I waited for a few minutes of silence until he came back.

"Here is your new access code. Are you ready to take it down?"

"Yes, go ahead."

"Good, your new access code number is 5 3 1 9 8 7. Voila! You should not have any problems. If you do, please call me back."

What a friendly guy, relaxed, cheerful, happy to help, I thought, a big improvement over the general unpleasant attitude of bank managers thirty years ago.

I was about to test the new access code number to open my account when something stopped me, a weird feeling about this number. I sat back in my desk chair, swiveling, rolling and gliding around on the wheels, staring out at the big cedar tree just outside the window over my desk, spacing out. What was it about this number?

I found myself moving like a sleepwalker to the kitchen, then standing on the deck, swaying from side to side, with the series of digits repeating itself—5 3 1 9 8 7—like a mantra, 5 3 1 9 8 7, on and on. I was in an altered state, a familiar place for me when I don't know what to do next.

Eventually, I walked back to my desk and saw the number I had written on the pad. This time, instead of seeing just random separate digits, I saw a configuration. I saw 1987, yes, that's it, the year 1987, and then I saw the other two digits fall into place: they could be the month and the day of the year 1987, and I read 5.3.1987.

May third, 1987, Gaby's date of birth. Eureka!

Was I dreaming? I could not believe that a bank manager in Paris had given to me, here in Berkeley, this perfect number. I made sure I was not fantasizing and opened my filing cabinet to find Gaby's birth certificate: yes, it was May 3, 1987, or 5.3.1987.

I wrote it in big numbers with a bright-orange felt pen on a white piece of cardboard, like this:

5 3 1 9 8 7

5 . 3 . 1987

and pinned it on the wall, at eye level, over my desk so I could stare at it. There it was, in front of me, facing me, there was no doubting it, it was the same number. This was real. I could not take my eyes away, hypnotized, my heart pounding.

What a blessing! I finally told myself, what a gift! Where did that come from?

Later I told Gaby about it. His reaction was laconic. "What are the chances?" he said, and he was not going to give it one more thought.

"Well, exactly, what are the chances? Zip, so how could such a thing happen?"

I was seized with pure bliss. I felt as if I had a sun shining inside my chest, and a little voice told me, "See the power of love. It created this little miracle. Never mind where it came from, just enjoy it!"

I am filled with wonder every time I look up and see this numinous sign, the six digits pinned on the wall. I see the play of consciousness! Divine playfulness, playing like the magical godson who came into my life, as the Petit Prince appeared to Saint-Exupéry in the Sahara desert, to remind me: keep playing, keep singing and dancing, keep loving and discovering joy.

Acknowledgments

I wish to thank the following individuals—in alphabetical order by last names—who have supported me in completing this Memoir: Claire Arnesen, Peggy Bendet, Sandy Boucher, Miriam Cantor, Susan Chasson, Ellie Cohen, Antoinette Constable, Mani Feniger, Susan Garratt, Nan Fink Gefen, Lisa Greenstein, Ann Jauregui, Molly Jones, Annie Kane, Shachi Katira, Claudia Lamoreaux, Nicole Liboiron, Joan Lohman, Monza Naff, Liz Raymer, Anais Salibian, Christine Schoeffer, Kendra Smith, Carolyn Zeiger.

About the Author

Odile Atthalin was born in Paris, France in 1936 to a patriarchal bourgeois family, the eldest of six children. After surviving the German Nazi Occupation in Normandy and the loss of a baby sibling, she witnessed D-Day and the liberation of her village by the American tanks. She majored in comparative literature at the Sorbonne and studied American Literature at Barnard College on a Fulbright Scholarship. Back in France she completed an M.A in Clinical Psychology. In 1969, she left for India, and kept traveling until 1983. Since 1988, she has maintained a private practice in Berkeley. In 1996, as a Senior Rosen Method Teacher, she founded the Rosen Method Open Center, a school to train Rosen Method Bodywork and Movement practitioners and teachers in the US and in Europe. In 1987, she became the godmother to a baby boy with special needs and became very involved in raising him. Atthalin loves reading and writing, in French and English. She finds great joy in meditation, yoga, Qi Gong, singing, hiking, dancing, and leading a weekly Movement class done to all kinds of good music.

Odile Atthalin is available for Rosen Method Bodywork Therapy including private treatments, supervisions, presentations and workshops. More information may be found at her website: www.rosenmethod-odile-atthalin.com. She can also be contacted at odile@lmi.net.

....

Gabriel Alexander Liboiron-Cohen, tenor, performer and vocal coach, may be contacted at: cohen.gabriel3@gmail.com.

Selected Titles from She Writes Press

She Writes Press is an independent publishing company
founded to serve women writers everywhere.
Visit us at www.shewritespress.com.

Make a Wish for Me: A Mother's Memoir by LeeAndra Chergey.
$16.95, 978-1-63152-828-6. A life-changing diagnosis teaches a
family that where's there is love there is hope—and that being
"normal" is not nearly as important as providing your child with
a life full of joy, love, and acceptance.

Rethinking Possible: A Memoir of Resilience by Rebecca Faye
Smith Galli. $16.95, 978-1-63152-220-8. After her brother's dev-
astatingly young death tears her world apart, Becky Galli embarks
upon a quest to recreate the sense of family she's lost—and learns
about healing and the transformational power of love over loss
along the way.

Changed By Chance: My Journey of Triumph Over Tragedy by
Elizabeth Barker. $16.95, 978-1-63152-810-1. When her dreams
of parenthood and becoming a career mom take a nightmarish
twist, Elizabeth Barker has to learn how to summon her inner
warrior—for her and her family's survival.

Filling Her Shoes: Memoir of an Inherited Family by Betsy Gra-
ziani Fasbinder. $16.95, 978-1-63152-198-0. A "sweet-bitter" story
of how, with tenderness as their guide, a family formed in the
wake of loss and learned that joy and grief can be entwined cohab-
itants in our lives.

A Leg to Stand On: An Amputee's Walk into Motherhood by
Colleen Haggerty. $16.95, 978-1-63152-923-8. Haggerty's candid
story of how she overcame the pain of losing a leg at seventeen—
and of terminating two pregnancies as a young woman—and
went on to become a mother, despite her fears.

*Blinded by Hope: One Mother's Journey Through Her Son's
Bipolar Illness and Addiction* by Meg McGuire. $16.95, 978-1-
63152-125-6. A fiercely candid memoir about one mother's roller
coaster ride through doubt and denial as she attempts to save her
son from substance abuse and bipolar illness.